MAX JAKOBSON

Finland: Myth and Reality

Otava
Publishing Company Ltd.
Helsinki

© 1987 Max Jakobson
Printed in Finland by Otava Printing Works,
Keuruu 1987

ISBN 951-1-08601-4

Contents

North Cape

Petsamo

Murmansk

1939

ARCTIC CIRCLE

Kemi

Oulu

U·S·S·R

Lieksa

Björko
Vaasa
Kuopio
Joensuu
1939

Tampere
Mikkeli
Sortavala
Pori
Kakisalmi
LAKE
Lahti
Viipuri
LADOGA

JAALAND
ISLANDS
Turku
HELSINKI
KARELIA

Hanko
HOGLAND
Porkkala
LENINGRAD
Jussaro I.

STOCKHOLM
Tallinn

ESTONIA

S W E D E N

F I N L A N D

GULF OF BOTHNIA

BALTIC SEA

Finland

•••••• Border 1939 —•—•— Border 1940

0   50   100   200   300 MILES

S·H·B

Foreword

Having spent the better part of my working life explaining Finland to foreigners, and sometimes to my countrymen themselves, I am alternately depressed and amused to find the Finland I encounter abroad, in the media and in conversation with well-informed people, still is largely a mythical country only remotely resembling present-day reality. Yet, in the case of Finland, I believe reality is stranger, and more exciting, than the myths. This is what I hope this book will show. It is not a systematic or comprehensive presentation of the country, but rather my personal view of how the Finnish experience relates to some of the central political issues of our time. One of these is, of course, the East-West relationship: a book about Finland is bound to be partly a book about the Soviet Union — and about the Russian tradition which is interwoven into the fabric of Soviet policy. But it must also be a book about the contest between two ideologies, about the role of cultural and social factors in economic development and, not least, about the enduring vitality of nationalism in an age of economic integration. In the past decades the supreme test for Finland has been to find a way to live in peace with her powerful neighbour without giving up her own system of government and her ties with the Western world. During the rest of the century the test is likely to be to secure Finland's place within the greater unity of Europe, a task that presents a new challenge to the independence and cultural identity of the Finnish nation. The outcome will depend on the ability of the Finns to continue to maintain the high degree of social cohesion and originality of national spirit they have shown in the past.

Helsinki, in May 1987
Max Jakobson

I
From Survival to Success

As history is written by the victors, so is the agenda
of world politics dictated by the powerful. The themes
and priorities of the international debate are set by a
handful of politicians, officials, editors and scholars in
half a dozen capitals: a form of cultural imperialism
which is not rendered any less effective by its being
unintended. The view of the world underlying influential analyses of international relations reflects primarily
the interests and aspirations of the great powers. Smaller nations are treated as objects of policy, statistical
units in categories of states classified in terms of their
relationship to their respective protectors or oppressors,
as ours and theirs — pawns to be gained or lost in the
conflicts or deals between the great powers.

In the case of Finland, the difficulty in gaining recognition and understanding on her own terms, as an
autonomous actor rather than a function of the policies
of others, is compounded by the language curtain that
conceals the innermost life of the Finnish people from
outsiders. Few foreign diplomats, journalists or scholars
know Finnish or Swedish, and only a fraction of the
texts needed for a comprehensive understanding of the
past and present of the Finnish people is available in
other languages. Much of the information about Finland available to foreigners is secondhand and second-
rate.

Only rarely during the last decades has Finland
surfaced above the horizon of international politics.

Former President Jimmy Carter was once asked how many times in his four years in office he had had to deal with a matter relating to Finland. After some thought he could recall one such occasion, but could not remember what it was about. In Henry Kissinger's account of his eight years at the center of policy-making — two volumes of a total of 2800 pages — Finland is mentioned once and then only as the place where President Ford met with Soviet leader Brezhnev in 1975.

I note this, not as a complaint about a lack of interest in Finland, but rather with relief. The agenda of urgent issues confronting the American president and his advisers is the sick list of the international community: only countries in trouble make it. The absence of any mention of Finland is proof of the success of her policy of neutrality — a policy designed to keep the country out of the quarrels between the big powers. But there is a price to pay: Those who make policy or influence opinion in the leading capitals of the world have no incentive to follow Finnish affairs. Their knowledge of Finland tends to be superficial and fragmentary.

As a result, Finland is forever at the mercy of the itinerant columnist who after lunch and cocktails in Helsinki is ready to pronounce himself upon the fate of the Finnish people. A person visiting, say, London for the first time, who does not know English and has only a vague notion of the significance of Dunkirk or the role of Winston Churchill, would hardly be regarded as qualified to comment on the British scene today. An equally profound ignorance about Finland is no deterrent. Obsessed as they usually are with one single aspect of the Finnish situation, relations with the Soviet Union, visitors from the West almost invariably produce a one-dimensional view of the country, corresponding to the current state of Western relations with the Soviet Union. Thus, in 1939–40, the Finns were idolized for their resistance against the Red Army; in 1941–44, ostracized for continuing to fight the Russians; at the end of the Second World War, castigated for their failure to heed Western advice to trust Moscow; in 1948, written off as lost for signing a treaty with the Soviet Union; and finally, at the present time, subjected to a kind of character assassination through the use of the term »Finlandization» to denote supine submission to Soviet domination.

It is commonplace to believe that the Finns live on the razor's edge, at the mercy of their powerful neighbour: in the words of a British observer, a nation »much admired, often pitied, never envied». Until quite recently, most Finns themselves were inclined to see themselves as a nation battling implacable Fate. The national ethos kept alive the 19th-century image of a country struggling to make a living in the cruel conditions of the Far North, an outpost of civilization, with a history that could be described as a series of narrow escapes from catastrophe, a people forever walking the tightrope without a safety net, with no hope of success beyond mere survival.

On their way to the 1980s, however, the Finnish people have acquired, without much conscious self-analysis, a new image of themselves as a people. They no longer feel they are living in the tragic situation of a lonely hero stoically facing powerful adversaries. In the speeches of politicians and the texts of social critics, Fate has been replaced by Fortune. Dag Hammarskjöld's dictum that to be born in Scandinavia is like receiving a winning ticket in life's lottery has been adopted by Finns as their new national motto. The survival of an independent Finland is taken for granted; the goal now is to create a successful society. Indeed, many Finns would claim this goal has already been reached, as is shown by an opinion poll conducted in the mid-80s, in which more than eight out of ten interviewed agreed with the statement that it is »a good fortune and a privilege» to be a Finn.

Success is of course an ambiguous concept. There is no agreed way to define or measure it. Just as in ancient Greece what Athens considered success was despised by Sparta, so today any claim of success put forward by one side in the ideological struggle of our time is rejected or ridiculed by the other. In a world divided by profound differences in values and priorities, success can only be perceived subjectively and described in relative terms. A nation is successful when a majority of its members, or just its leading elite, believes that its internal conditions or its position in the world are improving or, better still, that it is catching up with neighbours previously feared or envied, though in the eyes of outsiders it may still seem weak and poor.

Yet politicians and columnists do not hesitate to declare one nation a success and another a failure, as if the criteria for making such judgements were generally known and accepted. This is indeed the case, in a vague sort of way, among nations with similar values and roughly comparable economic standards. In the field of economic policy, the successes and failures of the rich industrial nations of the West and Japan are monitored by the Organization of Economic Cooperation and Development. The statistics issued by the OECD are like score cards from a never ending athletic contest in which medals are awarded to countries with high growth rates and low figures for inflation and unemployment.

Of course a nation needs more than a good OECD-rating to qualify as successful. To define what else is needed we would require a modern version of the Four

Freedoms proclaimed by President Franklin D. Roosevelt in 1941 as »the foundation of an ideal society». By joining together freedom of speech and religion with freedom from want and fear, Roosevelt attempted, perhaps without being aware of it, to marry two philosphical concepts of freedom: on the one hand the traditional political liberties of the individual designed to protect him against interference by the authorities, and on the other the economic and social rights which are given priority in collectivist societies.

The tension between the two concepts remains a central issue of our time. It has become far more complex than it seemed in Roosevelt's days. Old certainties have been clouded by new anxieties.

Freedom from fear, by which Roosevelt meant freedom from the fear of war, has become an overriding necessity in the nuclear age; how then are liberal societies to mount a credible defence against a ruthless totalitarian power? Freedom from want is the goal of every decent government, but the experiences of the 1970s have revealed the limits of collective action to achieve it.

In the Soviet Union, the »scientific truth» of Marxism- Leninism is being adjusted to economic realities. In China, Mao's little Red Book has been discarded. The Swedish Welfare State, publicized by Marquis Childs as the happy »Middle Way» between the social inequalities of capitalism and the lack of individual freedom under communism, has led into a dead end of oppressive taxation. The Yugoslav model of workers' self- rule has fallen into disrepute. The economic miracle of Japan, like the earlier German version, has revealed an unattractive underside of social tensions. None of the many creeds seems to offer a sure way to a happy balance between social security and individual initiative, equality and enterprise, political stability and revitalizing change. At the same time new problems unforeseen by Roosevelt demand attention: Should there be a fifth freedom – freedom from pollution? And what about freedom from terrorism and violent crime?

The Finnish claim of success is not based on the discovery of a new theory that others could apply. It is, rather, a triumph of pragmatism. The record, at any rate, is impressive.

In the 1980s Finland's national income per capita has passed that of Britain and France and is catching up with Sweden. International bankers have awarded the country with a Triple A-rating for creditworthyness. Within the OECD, Finland has been receiving frequent praise as a model pupil in the art of macro-economic management. Having for a quarter century successfully kept out of crises and conflicts, the Finnish people are beginning to acquire the smug sense of superiority characteristic of old-established neutral nations. Relations with the Soviet Union have become stable and predictable. In internal politics, a wide-ranging consensus has emerged across the dividing line between Right and Left. Militant Communism has dwindled to a fringe group. Failure in the 1960s and 1970s to catch up with Sweden in developing social services has turned out to be a blessing in the 1980s: as the public sector has remained around 40 % of GNP, the Finnish economy has been better able to respond to changing world conditions. A latecomer to industrialization Finland has also escaped some of its damaging consequences to nature and to the urban environment. In the World Human Rights Guide published by the Economist, Finland is given the top rating of 98 %, equalled only by Denmark, Netherlands and Sweden. Altogether, having for long felt themselves to be menaced by the East and let down by the West, the Finnish people today feel they are getting the best of both worlds.

The sense of security and well-being now enjoyed by the Finnish people may turn out to be illusory or ephemeral, to be blown away by some cold wind that could rise again in Europe in the future years. It is partly the product of a combination of fortunate circumstances — sheer good luck; partly it is due less to Finland's own achievements than to the failures of others. But credit must also be given to the political maturity and self-dicipline of the Finnish people and the good sense of its leaders, as well as to a system of government which combines a strong presidency with a peculiar brand of parliamentarism designed to encourage consensus and maintain stability in political life.

But what about Russia? A discussion about Finland usually turns into a discussion about her powerful Eastern neighbour. Few foreign observers are interested in Finland for her own sake; most of them hope to find in the Finnish experience a clue to the riddle of the Kremlin. When, in October 1961, in the course of preparations for an official visit of the Finnish President to the United States, I was questioned by the late President John F. Kennedy on various aspects of Finnish policy, it soon became obvious that what he really wanted to know was something about Soviet policy. »What puzzles us Americans», he said,»is why the Soviet Union has allowed Finland to retain her independence?»

Kennedy's question implied that in the natural scheme of things the Soviet Union surely must have wished to destroy Finnish independence, and if it has not done so, this must be due to some mysterious calculation on the part of Soviet leaders - most likely something designed to confuse and deceive the West. That the Finns themselves might have had something to do with maintaining their freedom is usually dismissed as naive.

The mystery arises, I believe, not from what actually has happened in Finland, but from the attempt to relate it to a general theory of what ought to have happened. George Kennan has written about »the persistent urge of Americans to seek universal formulae or doctrines» and »the tendency to divide the world neatly into Communist and free world components», rather than recognize the specific characteristics of each country. The inclination to generalize and search for categories is not confined to Americans. It is a universal human failing, and Finland is one of its victims. The political scientist is baffled by the Finnish case: none of the usual labels or cliches of international politics quite fits.

Finland claims to be a neutral country, yet is faithful to a pact which envisages the possibility of military cooperation with the Soviet Union; a Western democracy living, not in a state of permanent confrontation, but in apparent harmony with its Communist neighbour. This looks to some foreign observers like the Indian rope trick: a clever thing to do but not quite believable. Others, believing it, look upon Finland as a deserter from the never-ending struggle in defence of democracy. The Finnish example is sometimes held up as proof of the benefits of peaceful coexistence between Western democracies and the Soviet Union, at other times as a warning of the fate worse than death that awaits Western nations if they were foolish enough to follow the Finnish path. And from time to time the Finnish model is offered as a solution to the problems of Poland, or even Afghanistan.

The mystery about Finland resolves itself, I believe, when the historian is allowed to take over from the political scientist and developements in Finland are examined against the background of her own unique circumstances and experiences, not those of other countries with which Finland has never had much in common. The question to ask is not why the course of events in Finland has not been different from what it has been, but rather what forces and influences have in fact shaped it, including what the Finns themselves have done about it. The test of Finnish policy must be its results in Finnish terms, rather than its possible implications for East-West relations. Instead of asking whether it has been good or bad for the West, we must ask how it has served the freedom and well- being of the Finnish people.

II
The Russian Connection

A Finn talking about his country will almost invariably at some point remind his listeners that Finland is after all a small nation: a phrase pregnant with hidden meaning. It is sometimes said with pride: Look how much we have achieved although we are a small nation. Or it may be said defensively, by way of an alibi: You cannot expect too much from us, we are only a small nation.

The spirit of the phrase was brilliantly caught by Anthony Powell in his novel Venusberg (1932), in which a lady representing a fictional newly-independent small country – presumably Finland – tells a British diplomat: »We are only a little country. A little new country. You must not be surprised if sometimes we do not seem to do things so well as you big countries who have been big countires for so long. You big countries do not know what it is like to be a little country. . .»

Sometimes, however, humility is replaced by a smug tone of moral superiority, as if there were a special virtue attached to being a small nation; an assumption that once goaded Molotov, Stalin's Foreign Minister, to put down the Finnish Ambassador with the remark: »The fact that Finland is a small nation doesn't mean that you are always right.»

Molotov spoke more bluntly to the Foreign Minister of Lithuania in 1940: »You must be realistic enough to understand that the time of small nations has passed.» These words spelt the end of the independence of the Baltic states. But they also reveal more generally the essence of what it means to be a small nation. As defined by the Czech writer Milan Kundera,»the small nation is one whose very existence can be put in question at any moment: a small nation can disappear and it knows it». (The New York Review of Books, April 26, 1984.) The first business of a small nation is survival, as Poles remind themselves each time they sing the opening line of their national anthem: »Poland has not yet perished. . .»

It would be a mistake to believe that Kundera's definition could be confined to the small nations living in the shadow of Russian power. The view put forward by Molotov with such brutal candour was widely shared, though more gently expressed, in the West. At about the time the Red Army moved forward into the Baltic states in anticipation of the German onslaught, Winston Churchill urged the British Cabinet to take whatwever action necessary against the enemy, »without allowing the small nations to tie our hands».

In the aftermath of the Second World War the time of the small nations did indeed seem to have passed. The world was dominated by the overwhelming superiority of the United States of America. It was the only major power that had emerged from the war with its economy not only intact but vastly strenghtened. It was the sole possessor of nuclear weapons. It projected throughout the world its doctrines of liberal democracy, free enterprise and free trade. After a war fought against a racist enemy, the American ideology of One World, proclaiming the essential unity of mankind, carried a powerful appeal. Science and technology were already pointing the way to a global view of the world, and economic activity was evolving toward ever larger organizations extending across national bounda ries. Political development, it was generally believed, was bound to take the same direction. Smaller states were expected to merge into larger associations – a trend that was considered not only inevitable but also desiderable: Hitler had given nationalism a bad name. In the West, greater political unity ultimately leading to the creation of a United States of Europe was believed to be a necessary condition for the survival of democracy. In the East, the states in which the Communists held power had already merged – or so it seemed – into one vast empire ruled from Moscow.

We now know that the view of the world prevailing at the end of the Second World War was profoundly mistaken. Instead of an irresistible trend toward greater political unity, we have witnessed a continued fragmentation of political authority. There are now more small states than ever before in history. The membership of the United Nations has tripled in forty years. Stalin's great empire – the »Sino-Soviet bloc» –has broken up into several fractions. Nationalism has ceased to be a dirty word: no longer an agressive or expansionist doctrine, it has become the last defence of peoples against the anonymous forces of integration that threaten their identity. Contrary to beliefs widely held at the end of the Second World War, ideologies have failed to maintain an enduring hold of the loyalty of peoples: national interest has proved to be a stronger force than ideological commitment.

True, nationalism continues to be assailed from many sides – by Americans preaching the benefits of open markets, by Russians as masters of a multinational empire, by Communists believing in the primacy of the class struggle, by ecologists and other idealists who consider the division of mankind into nation states a primitive and irrational system. The nationalist policies of one's ally are deplored as narrow-minded and short-sighted, while similar tendencies in the other camp are applauded and encouraged. The fact remains, however, that nationalism is alive and well, on both sides of the dividing line between East and West: a phenomenon deserving renewed attention and study.

Once again, generalization is misleading: nationalism is by definition a belief in the unique, in contrast to the universal.

A small nation − one too weak to impose its will on others − establishes and preserves its identity by way of exclusion or rejection, by saying no to assimilation. Finland is a case in point.

The independence of Finland was declared in December in 1917, but the birth of the nation took place a century earlier. The first essential step was not, as is commonly believed, freedom from Russian rule, but separation from Sweden. This came about as a minor byproduct of the deal struck between Napoleon and Alexander I in 1807, in which the Russian Czar undertook to persuade or, if necessary, compell Sweden to join Napoleon's blockade against Britain.

The image of the meeting between the two Emperors at Tilsit is engraved upon the collective memory of the Finnish people, just as is that of the Foreign Ministers of the Soviet Union and Nazi Germany meeting in August 1939 to carve up Eastern Europe into what euphemistically was called spheres of influence: two vivid lessons in Realpolitik which have fostered among Finns a disillusioned view of the nature of international relations and an instinct for taking evasive action.

Paradoxically − or so it may seem today − it was the Russian conquest of Finland in 1808 that created the conditions in which a Finnish nation could emerge and ultimately gain independence. As part of the Kingdom of Sweden, Finland had been a poor and neglected province, a »developing region» we would call it today, with no political or cultural identity of its own. The language of education and administration was Swedish; for a Finn the only road to advancement was by way of assimilation into Swedish culture. Had Finland remained part of Sweden, the Finnish- speaking population, or whatever would be left of it, might today be one of the many frustrated linguistic minorities that angrily clamour for recognition.

Having nonetheless fought valiantly against the Russian invaders, the Finnish people found that the switch of allegiance they were forced to accept was rewarded with an enhanced political status. Alexander I was at the time still influenced by the liberal ideas of the Enlightenment. He was also anxious to gain the loyalty of his new Finnish subjects. In spring 1809 he convened the representatives of the the Four Estates (clergy, nobility, burghers and peasants) confirming their rights and privileges. The Grand Duchy of Finland was to keep its Swedish laws and administrative institutions. Finland, the Czar declared, was »elevated as a nation to the ranks of nations».

The meaning of the word nation must be understood in the context of the time. Many nations dwelled in the vast house of the Russian Czar: Finland was to be one of them. Yet the compact concluded between the Emperor and his Finnish subjects was unique in the sense that as Grand Duke of Finland the ruler of Russia, an autocrat with absolute power in the rest of his empire, accepted the role of a constitutional monarch. For Finns it became a holy covenant and the basis of their autonomy.

Finland was run at the time by a narrow elite of nobles and a few educated burghers. But unlike Poland, for instance, Finland was already then a relatively egalitarian society. There were no great nobles, no vast estates, no serfs. The typical Finnish nobleman of the early part of the 19th century was a former officer of the Swedish army who farmed a modest sized estate. The nobility had a long- established tradition of public service. Many of the educated Finns of that time were drawn to St. Petersburg, a great European centre open to talent from every part of the empire. The Russian army in particular attracted young Finns, many of whom attained the highest ranks – among them Carl Gustav Mannerheim who later was to play a leading role in the attainment and defence of Finnish independence.

The compact of 1809 did not by itself make Finland a nation – a nation in the modern sense. But Finland did aquire in 1809 a territorial identity and a separate administrative structure. Unlike many other peoples, the Finns never became a nation in search of a state. Finnish nationalism as it developed during the 19th century flowed into a ready-made mould. The romanticism characteristic of nationalist movements elsewhere was tempered by the mundane tasks of administration.

A nation is made not born. Nationhood is a frame of mind. A tribe, or an ethnic entity, is transformed into a nation by the developement of a consciousness of a shared past and a common destiny. Such a consciousness can only be created by the historians and poets, artists and composers. A nation must have a cultural identity – a term that implies the existence within the group itself of the kind of cohesion and unity that outsiders are able to recognize as something distinct and singular. Without its cultural fingerprints political autonomy remains an empty shell, as can be seen in so many states in former colonial territories in the Third World.

In the cultural sense,the emerging Finnish nation in

the 19th century had a natural eastern border. Lutheran Finland with its western values and a legal system and administrative structure inherited from Sweden had no difficulty in marking its separateness from orthodox Russia living under autocratic rule. In the west, however, the line was blurred. Through the continued dominance of the Swedish language, Finland was rendered a split personality: politically part of the Russian empire, but culturally still linked to the old motherland. The issue of language thus acquired a decisive significance in the development of a Finnish nation. »Has a nation anything more precious than the language of its fathers?» asked Herder, the prophet of European nationalism. »In it dwell its entire world of tradition, history, religion, principles of existence, its whole heart and soul.» The publication in 1835 of the Kalevala, one of the great epics of mankind, infused the Finnish people with pride in their cultural heritage; it also made the Finnish claim to nationhood widely known in the civilized world. The drive to develop Finnish, spoken by the majority, into a modern language became the centerpiece of Finnish nationalism. In the 1860's Finnish was finally granted by law equal status with Swedish as an official language. Paradoxically this was due to the efforts of members of the ruling elite who abandoned Swedish and adopted Finnish, a language unrelated to the Indo-European languages. (It belongs to the Fenno-Ugrian group of languages represented in Europe by Estonian and Hungarian). Many also changed their family names from Swedish to Finnish: a collective act of linguistic conversion comparable to the adoption of Hebrew by the Zionist settlers of Palestine.»We are no longer Swedes, we do not want to become Russians, so let us be Finns»: this was the simple credo of the founding fathers of Finnish nationalism.

Finland has remained a bilingual country, and the Swedish language still today serves as an invaluable link with the other Nordic countries. (Today a little over 6 % of the population speak Swedish as their mother tongue, but a large proportion of the Finnish-speakers have some knowledge of Swedish and some are bilingual.) But it is hard to imagine that the Finnish people could have maintained genuine political independence without their separate linguistic identity. Language has acted like a protective cocoon that has made the Finns resistant to foreign influences and assimilation.

The men who ran Finland in the 19th century found that loyalty to the ruler payed off in terms of freedom of action in internal matters. They kept what today would be called a low profile, avoiding any challenge to Russian security or prestige. They learned through practice the subtle art of steering Finnish autonomy past potential points of conflict with the vital interests of the empire. They cultivated a conservative social outlook, shielding the Finnish people from the influence of liberal currents of thought that might disturb the Russian autocracy. »Leave the Finns alone,» Czar Nicolas I is said to have told his ministers at the time of the Polish uprising in 1830. »It is the only part of my realm which never has given us any trouble.»

The interplay between Polish rebelliousness and Finnish caution continued. At the time of the second Polish uprising in 1863 the Finnish philosopher-statesman J.W. Snellman warned his countrymen against siding openly with Poland against Russia: Such foolish gestures would only hurt Finland without any benefit to the poor Poles. Finnish loyalty was promptly rewarded. Alexander II made Finland a show-case of his liberal ideas. During his reign Finnish self-government took a great leap forward. His statue still stands in the central square of Helsinki.

Toward the end of the 19th century the Russian attitude to Finland began to change. The Russian military leaders, obsessed by the German danger, were dismayed to discover on the doorsteps of St. Petersburg a part of the empire which had developed into a foreign country. Finns were described in their passports as »Finnish citizens and Russian subjects». Finland had her own laws and legislature, her own civil service and judiciary, her own currency and customs tariffs, even her own army for the defence of Finnish territory. The Finnish people enjoyed a higher standard of living than the rest of the empire, a fact that aroused a great deal of resentment among Russians. Finland, it was said, took advantage of the security provided by the empire without paying for it.

The Finnish system of constitutional government came under increasing criticism from Russian conservatives determined to defend autocracy at home. What under Alexander II had been a show-case of liberalism turned under Nicholas II into a dangerous precedent. It encouraged separatism in other parts of the empire and demands for constitutional reform in Russia herself. By the end of the century the Czar and his leading advisers had become determined to restrict Finnish autonomy and integrate Finland militarily and administratively into the Russian system: to relegate the country to the status of a Baltic province.

After almost a century of peaceful coexistence, the relationship between Russia and Finland was transformed into a classical confrontation between a great power bent upon safeguarding its imperial interests and a small nation fighting for its own way of life. The Finnish people at first could not believe that their Grand Duke, the Russian Czar, could break his solemn pledge to respect the Finnish constitution: surely he must have been misled by his advisers. More than half a million Finns signed an address appealing to the Emperor, but he refused to receive it. A mood of defiance, eloquently expressed in Jean Sibelius' Finlandia, spread among the Finnish people. Artists and writers were in the frontline in defence of what was perceived to be a threat to the very essence of Finland's national identity.

The Western world for the first time became aware of the Finnish national struggle. The Finnish pavillion at the Paris World Fair in 1900, designed by Eliel Saarinen, the first in a line of great Finnish architects, received wide attention. More than a thousand distinguished Europeans signed an appeal on behalf of Finland's autonomy, but it was of course rejected by the Emperor as interference in Russian internal affairs.

The Russian policy of repression was met with a campaign of civil disobedience. Recalcitrant civil servants and judges were being dismissed, prominent Finnish leaders banished to Siberia or forced into exile, and many young men emigrated to America to avoid conscription into the Russian army. As Russian pressure mounted, an agonizing debate went on between the conservatives who advocated appeasement of Russian power and prestige as the only means of preserving the essence of Finnish national life, and the liberal constitutionalists who insisted on standing fast on legal rights regardless of the consequences. There were also the activists who prepared for direct action by sending young men to Germany for military training; and the left-wing revolutionaries who made common cause with their Russian comrades in the belief that the overthrow of the Czarist regime would bring both national liberation and social reform. It was a debate that has a timeless quality: the arguments used then could be applied today wherever nations face the cruel choice between submitting to superior power and engaging in suicidal resistance.

The methods employed by the Czarist authorities at the time seem amateurish by the high standards in the art of repression achieved in the 20th century. There were no executions, no mass terror, no concentration camps. When a member of the Mannerheim family was forced into exile, he was given a week to put his affairs in order, which at the time was considered harsh treatment, but it did enable his brother Carl Gustav, then a colonel in the Chevalier Guards in St. Petersburg, to travel to Helsinki to bid his brother farewell before he sailed off to Stockholm. Yet the final outcome did not seem in doubt. It was put in two words by a Russian writer: Finis Finlandiae!

Passive resistance did, however, gain time, often the most precious asset for a small nation under pressure. In the end Finland was rescued by the Russian defeat in Japan and spreading unrest in Russia herself. Russian policy in Finland lurched from repression to reform, then back again to repression, until the collapse of the Czarist regime provided Finland with the opportunity to declare full independence on December 6th, 1917.

This date was neither an end nor a beginning: rather a high point in a continuing process. Lenin's government was the first to recognize the independence of Finland on the last day of 1917, but forty thousand Russian troops remained in Finland and the Bolsheviks were suspected of relying on the advance of the revolution to bring back to the Soviet Union what had been lost by old Russia. In January 1918 the »Red Guards» of the Finnish working class seized power in Helsinki, and the government entrusted General Mannerheim, who had returned to his native Finland after thirty years of service under the Czars, with the task of organizing a »White Army» to restore order. The war between the Reds and the Whites was as cruel as civil wars usually are, and before it had come to an end some three months later, a German expeditionary force had landed in Southern Finland to ensure the victory of the Whites. A formal peace treaty with Soviet Russia was concluded in 1920.

The legacy of Finland's Russian connection was in many ways contradictory. Direct Russian cultural influence remained marginal; knowledge of the Russian language, for instance, was always limited. (Today it is negligible: less than 1 % of the students in secondary schools choose to study Russian, while more than 80 % take English as their first foreign language.) The change of regime that had taken place in Russia in 1919 did not erase memories of Czarist oppression. The generation of Finns who had grown up in the beginning of the century regarded Russia, Communist or otherwise, as the permanent enemy of Finland's freedom. The militant nationalists of the young Republic rejected not only Communism but all things Russian.

After the Second World War a broader interpretation of Finnish history has prevailed. The 19th century is now often described as a golden age in which Finnish national aspirations and Russian security interests were successfully harmonized. The influences received from the East are today acknowledged to have enriched Finnish cultural life. The feeling of hostility and fear has virtually disappeared. Young Finns today view the Soviet Union with a greater detachment than probably other Westerners. Yet, in spite of the never-ending shuttle of official delegations and the steady flow of tourists on guided tours, Russia on the whole remains to most Finns an alien country.

On the Russian side, policy toward Finland can only

be understood within a wider context of imperial interests, then and now. A preoccupation with security runs from Peter the Great all the way across the divide of the Bolshevik Revolution to Stalin and his successors. The events of 1917- 18 could be taken to confirm the worst fears of the Russian generals who had warned that Finnish separatism would open the gates to a German attack on St. Petersburg. But it could also be argued that the attempt to suppress Finnish national self-determination had created the enemy it had been designed to keep out, and that the advice of Nicholas I — »leave the Finns alone» — had achieved for almost a century maximum security at minimum cost.

Historical analogies must not be pressed too far, but obviously the present relations between Finland and the Soviet Union have been influenced, on both sides, by patterns of behaviour and thought that have been shaped by past associations. The Finns have learned to live with the ebb and flow of Russian power. The Russians who run the Soviet Union have learned — so it would seem at the time of writing — to accept the independence of Finland as a fact of contemporary life. But two more wars and several other tests of will and cunning were needed before harmony could be restored.

III
The Winter War

The balance of power — the »correlation of forces», as Soviet analysts would say — between a big power with world-wide interests and commitments and a small nation with the single objective of survival cannot be calculated by simple arithmetic. It is an equation which the leaders of big powers seem incapable of solving, as has been demonstrated in Vietnam and Afghanistan. The Soviet invasion of Finland in 1939 — the Winter War — should have been a useful lesson.

The story can be simply told. In October 1939 the Finnish government was invited to send a delegation to Moscow to discuss »concrete political questions». Stalin himself explained to the Finns what these were. He said he needed more depth for the defence of Leningrad and this could be obtained only at the expense of Finland. The Finnish border had to be moved farther north from the city and the Soviet navy had to have a base on the southern coast of Finland close to Helsinki.

Stalin's demands were made in the shadow of his agreement with Hitler giving the Soviet government a free hand in the eastern part of the Baltic. The three Baltic states — Estonia, Latvia and Lithuania — had already given in to similar Soviet demands. Berlin advised the Finns to do the same. Stockholm told them not to expect military aid from Sweden. London and Paris were uninterested, realizing that the base Stalin wanted could only be used against Germany. Washington remained neutral. The Finnish leaders knew they stood alone, and they agreed to give up some territory north of Leningrad. But they refused to yield the base Stalin asked for, fearing it might be used to subvert Finnish independence.

On this issue the talks in Moscow broke down, and at the end of November 1939 Stalin launched his attack. For a hundred winter days the Finns held out, but in the end they had to make peace on terms that were worse than the ones they had rejected before the attack. Stalin got the base he wanted as well as a great deal more territory than he had originally demanded.

A trivial tale in the context of world history: throughout the ages bloody skirmishes have been fought along the edges of empires. In the vast drama of the Second World War, the Soviet-Finnish conflict was merely an incident within an episode, a local Soviet campaign to move by force a recalcitrant pawn into the square assigned to it in the deal between Stalin and Hitler.

Yet the Winter War is remembered, or rather half remembered like a legend from a distant time, more widely than many larger campaigns that had a more direct bearing on the outcome of the struggle between the great powers. Its emotional impact, at the time, was immense. The Finnish stand against overwhelming odds offered the Western world a cause without blemish: the Finns defended democracy and freedom and justice, all the things the Western democracies believed in but had had at the time little chance actually to fight for. A vast reservoir of frustrated idealism was released into a flood of sympathy for Finland. Volunteers offered themselves from as far away as Abessinia. Kermit Roosevelt, son of the late President Theodore Roosevelt, announced the formation of an international brigade. In Britain, the roll of volunteer units to be sent to Finland read like extracts from Debrett :anyone who had ever spent a skiing holiday in St. Moritz was qualified. Robert Sherwood was inspired to write »There shall be no night». President Roosevelt spoke of »the rape of Finland» and Churchill called the Soviet invasion »a despicable crime against a noble people». In France the government ordered the Soviet trade mission to be closed, Italy recalled her ambassador from Moscow. And a message of encouragement from Uruguay was solemnly read in the Finnish Parliament.

The Finnish people, having had no previous experience of being the center of world attention, were dazzled by the etravagant expressions of sympathy and admiration. Like simple country folk who take the polite phrases of society literally, they were led to believe that practically the entire civilized world was on the point of rushing to their aid. Perhaps this was a useful self-deception; for what Finns in those days needed most was faith and hope, and to sustain them it was necessary to believe that a rescue party was on its way. As a result the word »sympathy» later acquired an ironic twist in the Finnish language.

On another plane, too, the Winter War had an impact far wider than its military limits. Its political repercussions ranged from a crisis in German-Italian relations to the fall of the Daladier government in France. It roused the League of Nations from its deathbed to expel the Soviet Union. It brought neutral Sweden to the very edge of war and helped to breach the isolation of the United States. It sent the Allied governments on what Lord Alanbrooke has called a wild goose chase for a new front in the North. It inspired French schemes of knocking the Soviet giant off its clay feet. It was an incident that almost unhinged the power alignments in the Second World War.

The outcome of the Winter War continues to mystify

historians. According to one popular myth Finland's survival was the result of Stalin's sentimental attachment to the place where he had met Lenin for the first time. (This happened at a clandestine party conference in 1906.) Even Isaac Deutscher, in his celebrated biography of Stalin, wrote of the Soviet dictator's »exceptional mildness» towards Finland.

No such psycho-historical explanations are necessary for understanding Soviet policy in 1939. Stalin's demands were neither original nor unexpected. Already Peter the Great had said that »the ladies of St. Petersburgh could not sleep peacefully» so long as Finland remained in enemy hands. Stalin's said the same thing in less elegant language. The enemy he feared was Germany. The Finnish negotiators tried to convince him that Finland was determined to remain neutral and would resist any German attempt to use Finnish territory for an attack against the Soviet Union. Such assurances Stalin brushed aside with the remark: »They will not ask you, they will come anyway.» But the Red Army, he said, would not remain behind its own borders waiting for the onslaught. It would move forward to meet the enemy.

Stalin's demands for more territory north of Leningrad and a naval base at the mouth of the Gulf of Finland had been lifted straight out of the archives of the Czarist general staff. Indeed, he explicitly referred to Czarist precedents in support of his claim.

None of this came as a surprise to the Finnish government. In the peace talks of 1920 the Soviet side had argued for frontiers that would provide greater depth to the defence of Leningrad, but at the time Lenin's newly founded state had been too weak to enforce its claims. During 1938 and again in spring 1939 secret Soviet emissaries had made soundings in Helsinki along similar lines, but to no avail.

But now Stalin himself had spoken, and the Finnish leaders were faced with the full weight of Soviet power. They conceded that the Soviet Union had a legitimate concern with regard to the security of Leningrad and were willing to accept a frontier adjustment north of the city as well as to cede a number of islands in the Gulf of Finland. But they balked at permitting the Soviet navy to establish a base at Hanko on the southern shore of the Gulf at a distance of 65 miles from the Finnish capital. They distrusted Soviet intentions: the base demanded by Stalin might be used to force Finland into servitude. But even accepting at face value Stalin's assurance that the base was needed solely for the purpose of defending Leningrad against intrusions from other big powers, its effect would have been to destroy the credibility of Finnish neutrality. In anticipation of a German-Soviet clash Finnish foreign policy had laboured for years to dissociate Finland from Nazi Germany and gain for her international recognition as a Scandinavian neutral. The goal of Finnish policy was to keep the country out of the coming storm, not to seek protection from either side.

Stalin's demand for a naval base was the issue on which the Finnish-Soviet talks broke down in November 1939. Yet hardly anyone believed that the Soviet Union would go to war. Military experts argued that a winter campaign against Finland could not possibly serve Soviet interests. They were of course quite right, but they failed to foresee Stalin's blunder. The Red Army struck on November 30, 1939, at the onset of one of the severest winters of the 20th century.

On that same day it was revealed in Moscow that the Red Army had received its marching orders in response to a request for aid from »the democratic government of Finland», a fictional body composed of Finnish Communists in exile and headed by O.W.Kuusinen, a former leader of the Reds in the Finnish civil war, who had fled to Russia in 1918 and there risen to a prominent position in the Comintern, the organ directing the world Communist movement.

Setting up puppet governments had been standard Soviet practice in the various operations carried out in the beginning of the 1920s to recover territories that had been part of the Czarist empire but had seceded during the turmoil of the revolution and civil war. Kuusinen's job was to provide a fig- leaf to cover what the rest of the world considered naked aggression.

But if the Soviet leaders believed that the Kuusinen government might rally the Finnish workers to the side of the invaders, they had utterly misread the mood of the Finnish people. The civil war of 1918 could no longer be rekindled. Whatever internal differences and doubts had existed were wiped out by the open challenge to Finnish sovereignty. The question whether more concessions ought to have been offered to avoid war became irrelevant: the Soviet Union recognized only the Kuusinen government and rejected all attempts to resume negociations. The choice was between fighting and unconditional surrender.

The conduct of the initial Soviet operations indicates that Moscow expected an easy march to Helsinki. So did the rest of the world. But Finnish forces, though heavily outnumbered, succeeded in stopping the Soviet advance on the Karelian Isthmus. Along the long eastern border large columns of invaders were totally annihilated. By Christmas the entire Soviet offensive had bogged down. Stalin was forced to reassess the situation. At the beginning of January 1940 a complete reorganization of Soviet forces was undertaken and reinforcements were brought in.

The British and French governments also did some rethinking. At first they had been reluctant to get involved in a struggle that seemed doomed to fail. But the initial success of Finland's defence had changed their minds. The Allied governments were under pressure from public opinion to do something to save Finland. A northern expedition was judged not only to be a popular move but also to offer a chance to hit at Germany from a new direction. On their way to Finland the Allied forces could take over control of the Norwegian coast and occupy Sweden's iron ore mines. With such goals in mind the Supreme War Council decided in the beginning of February 1940 to send an expeditionary force to Scandinavia, provided Finland appealed for aid.

In retrospect, the Allied plan seems almost farcically inept. The troops assigned to the Northern adventure were pitifully inadequate. They could not have saved Finland. Nor is it likely that Hitler would have stood idly by while the Allied occupied northern Norway and Sweden. The whole of Scandinavia would have been plunged into war, with disastrous consequences all round.

Yet the Allied plan did help Finland – so long as it was not carried out. It probably induced the Soviet government to reconsider its Finnish policy. Stalin's declared purpose was to keep the Soviet Union out of the war between Germany and the West. The success of this policy was endangered by the Finnish campaign, which threatened to involve Soviet forces in a clash with the Allies. At the beginning of February 1940 the Soviet government let it be known through Stockholm that it was prepared to resume negociations with the Finnish government. Kuusinen was no longer mentioned. For the Finns, this was a momentous victory. From then on the war was no longer about Finland's independence; it was about territory – a negociable issue.

But Soviet prestige was now in need of repair: the peace terms were far in excess of Stalin's original demands. In addition to the base at Hanko and the islands in the Gulf of Finland, Finland was asked to cede the entire province of Viipuri up to what had been the frontier of Peter the Great: once again Stalin explicitly invoked this historical precedent. To back up this demand Soviet forces in February began a new offensive on the Karelian Isthmus, far more powerful and more skillfully led than in December; the Finnish defence line on the road to Viipuri was soon broken.

Throughout February and in the first week of March the Finnish government was torn between the uncertainties of Allied aid and the awful prospect of peace on Soviet terms. London and Paris kept pressing the Finns to appeal for aid. Never before in history had two great powers so insistently urged a small nation fighting for its life to accept their rescue mission. The Allied troops were already waiting in their ships: all that was needed was a signal from Helsinki. Yet in the end the Finnish government decided to reject the offer of aid and make peace on terms that meant ceding to the enemy more territory than up to then had been given up by the army.

That it was a wise decision cannot be doubted. It was based on the cool appraisal of Marshal Mannerheim and his generals who realized that Allied help would be too late and too little. But it was also an expression of a deep-seated reluctance on the part of the Finnish political leaders to leave the fate of the nation in the hands of the great powers.

IV
The Second Round

The real significance of the Winter War was not widely understood at the time. The spotlight quickly moved to new campaigns, fresh tragedies. Finland once again sank below the news horizon of the international media. Soon enough »There shall be no night» was again being played to full houses — with Greece as the scene of the action.

In reality, however, the Winter War was only the first act in the Finnish-Soviet drama. The peace treaty which was signed in Moscow in March 1940 was supposed to create »precise conditions of reciprocal security» between Finland and the Soviet Union. In fact the end of fighting was followed by an intense war of nerves. Soviet pressure to prevent closer ties between Finland and Sweden and interference in Finnish domestic politics created in Finland the suspicion that Moscow was determined to complete by subversion the task it had failed to carry through by military means. The fate of the Baltic states which were annexed by the Soviet Union in summer 1940 sharpened Finnish anxieties. In November 1940 ominous information of Soviet intentions was received from Berlin where, according to German records, Molotov had told Hitler that the Soviet government intended »to solve the Finnish question» in the manner it had applied to Bessarabia and the Baltic states.

In this situation the Finnish responded with relief to the first hint of support from Germany, the only power which in 1940 could provide a counterweight to Soviet pressure. This came in August 1940, when Hitler had begun his preparations for his attack against the Soviet Union. Finland was offered the chance of bying arms from Germany in return for allowing German troops to pass through Finland to Norway. Sweden had already agreed to a similar German request, while Finland has just granted the Soviet Union the right of transit to the Hanko base. At the time the Finnish- German transit agreement seemed a useful bargaining chip. In fact it proved to be the point of no return for Finnish policy. It was the first step in a systematic German campaign to tie Finland to Hitler's war plans. The transit agreement was in reality a cover for the future movement of German troops from Norway, not back to Germany, but into the Soviet Union. On June 22, 1941, the day the German invasion of the Soviet Union was set in motion, Hitler announced that in the North his troops stood »side by side» with their Finnish comrades-in-arms.

In a formal sense, the Finnish government was still uncommitted, and its first reaction to Hitler's announcement was to declare its neutrality. But this lacked credibility. There had been collusion between the Finnish and German military leaders. A strong opinion in Finland welcomed the German invasion as an opportunity to recover what had been lost in 1940, or even to create a »greater Finland» including the Finnish-speaking Karelians living under Soviet rule. In any case, with German troops in Lapland poised for attack and Soviet forces in their base in Hanko, neutrality could not have been maintained for long. In fact it lasted four days. On June 25, the Soviet Union launched air attacks against targets on Finnish territory, and in the evening of that day the Finnish government declared that the country was at war with the Soviet Union.

By joining Hitler's war against the Soviet Union Finland had acted according to the Macchiavellian principle »that for the purpose of saving the country no proposition ought to be rejected. . . the defence of the country is always good no matter whether effected by honourable or ignominious means». But the Finns used a long spoon to sup with the devil. Finnish policy was to insist that Finland was waging a separate war, coinciding with but not part of the German-Soviet struggle. It was called the »Continuation War» − the second round of the conflict that had opened in November 1939. Finland was not an ally of Germany: she was a cobelligerent. She was not a German satellite: Nazi ideology made no headway in Finland and German attempts to impose it were firmly rejected. (Thus Finland never discriminated against its Jewish citizens.) The conduct of Finnish military operations was also designed to underline the separate character of Finland's war. After recapturing the territory lost in 1940 the Finnish troops moved into Soviet Karelia to establish a defensive line along the Svir River connecting Lake Onega with Lake Ladoga. But there they stopped , and German requests for Finnish participation in the offensive against Leningrad or the Murmansk railway were refused.

The finer points of the Finnish case were lost on public opinion, or even on most governments, on either side of the Second World War. Cobelligerency was a concept too sophisticated to make much impression on nations engaged in a fight for their lives. Germans tended to look upon Finland as an ally. In Western countries, she was regarded as a friend of the enemy. The vast fund of sympathy and admiration for Finland created by the Winter War was largely dissipated. Yet the distinctive character of the Finnish- Soviet conflict was recognized by the United States government, which refrained from declaring war on Finland.

»Every war must end»: the title of Fred Iklé's book (Columbia University Press 1971) contains a banal truth which often puts statesmanship to its severest test. After the German defeat at Stalingrad in January 1943 the Finnish government decided it had to find a way to end the war against the Soviet Union. But how and when? Timing was the crucial issue. To make the move too early would risk German retaliation; to leave it too late would mean going down with Hitler.

Peace feelers put out in the beginning of 1943 provoked German threats of »extreme action». A year later Finnish emissaries went to Moscow to find out on what terms peace could be concluded, but the Soviet demands were rejected as too harsh. At the time the Finnish army still stood along the Svir River, deep in Soviet territory. The Finnish leaders hoped to use this »position of strength» to gain a better bargain.

This proved to be an illusion. On 9th June 1944, as the Allies were landing in Normandy, more that twenty Soviet infantry divisions, under cover of one of the most devastating artillery barrages of the Second World War and backed by more than four hundred combat planes, launched an offensive against the Finnish lines on the narrow front of the Karelian Isthmus. They broke through on the western shore along the road to Viipuri; the Finnish forces had to withdraw all along the Isthmus, and from Soviet Karelia as well, to avoid encirclement. A Finnish request for peace talks was met with a Soviet demand for surrender. At the same time Germany offered military assistance on condition that Finland commit herself not to make a separate peace. The choice was between surrender and a fight to the bitter end.

The dilemma was resolved by the Finnish President, Risto Ryti, who gave the pledge required by the Germans in the form of a personal letter addressed to Hitler. He thus deliberately exceeded his constitutional powers so as to avoid committing the Finnish government. His personal word was enough for the Germans who sent both troops and arms to the Karelian Isthmus. The German troops were of little use, but the modern weapons received from Germany were important. By the middle of July the Soviet offensive was stopped before it had reached the 1940 border. The Finnish army was severely bloodied but still unbeaten.

Once again Finnish resistance succeeded in raising the cost of conquest beyond what the Soviet leaders were prepared to invest on a peripheral front. Soviet military historians have revealed that the objective of the offensive begun in June 1944 was the occupation of southern Finland. But once it had been stopped Stalin ordered his troops to regroup for defence. He needed his crack divisions more urgently elsewhere — for the race to Berlin.

The time gained by Finland was of decisive value. Germany, hard pressed on two fronts, could no longer retaliate effectively. In the beginning of August Ryti resigned and was replaced by Marshal Mannerheim. The new President informed Hitler that he did not regard Ryti's pledge as binding. Stalin on his part no longer insisted on surrender: thus Moscow, too, implicitly recognized the separate character of the Finnish war. On 19 September 1944 an armistice agreement was finally signed in Moscow.

The peace terms restored the frontier of 1940, except in the Far North where the Soviet Union annexed Petsamo with its valuable nickel mines and its ice-free port on the Arctic. A Soviet naval base was again established on the southern coast of Finland, this time on the peninsula of Porkkala, which is even closer to Helsinki than is Hanko. Finland had to undertake to pay a war indemnity to the Soviet Union in the form of industrial goods and to hand over all former German assets. The Finnish merchant marine had to be placed at the disposal of the Allied powers. Finland also had to drive out the German troops, 200 000 men strong, from Lapland, and it took a campaign of six months to force them to withdraw across the Artic frontier into Norway. On their way they laid waste the entire province of Lapland: this was Hitler's revenge for Finland's treachery, as he called it, in making peace before Germany's final doom.

The entire population of the area ceded to the Soviet Union — more than 400 000 people — had chosen to leave their homes rather than live under Soviet rule: they had to be resettled. An Allied Control Commission, in which the Soviet element was dominant, had been installed in Helsinki to supervise the implementation of the Armistice Agreement. The Communist Party had been legalized and was feeding on the misery and suffering caused by three and a half years of fighting. The Western powers, still engaged in the last phase of their struggle against Germany, had no interest in the fate of a small nation that in their view had taken the wrong turn.

V
Victory in Defeat

Finland had lost the war, it was said. And this is of course true, if the Finnish-Soviet conflict is seen as a traditional war over land and frontiers. But to take such a view would be to miss the point. Finland was defeated. But she was not conquered. Apart from Great Britain and the Soviet Union, Finland was the only one of all the European nations involved in the Second World War to avert an enemy occupation. Her social fabric remained intact and the continuity of her political institutions unbroken. In this fact lies an achievement that transcends the conventional meaning of such terms as defeat or victory. For in the end Finland did not fight for Karelia or Hanko. She did not fight for any abstract priciples or ideals. She fought for national survival. When the fight was over, Finland was a nation crippled and exhausted. But Finland survived. This may seem a pitifully unheroic end to a story of so much effort and sacrifice, suffering and blood. But for a small nation, in the iron times of the Second World War, survival was a rare triumph.

The price paid was heavy. Finland lost 87 000 men in 1939-45, 2,3 % of the population. Every village has its war memorial. André Malraux, during a visit to Finland as French Minister of Culture in 1963, was taken to see the war graves in a rural cemetery and told how every soldier killed in action whose body could be found was taken home to be buried. Visibly moved, Malraux exclaimed: »Enfin un peuple civilisé!»

A civilized people: not only because it honours those who have sacrificed their lives for the nation's freedom, but also because it had the wisdom to stop fighting in time. »Only uncivilized tribes fight to the last man,» wrote J.W. Snellman, more than a hundred years ago. A civilized nation, he wrote, is conscious of its duty to bend itself to external necessity in order to safeguard its own future, to rely only on its own resources, and to desire and seek only what it can achieve and maintain by its own strength.

In similar terms Mannerheim addressed Hitler in August 1944: »Germany will live on, even if fate should deny you victory in your fighting. Nobody can give such an assurance regarding Finland. If this nation of barely four million be defeated militarily, there can be no doubt that it will be driven into exile or exterminated. I cannot expose my people to such a risk.»

But could war had been avoided altogether by a more conciliatory policy in 1939? It has, after all, been possible since the end of the war to reconcile the independence of Finland as a Western democracy with the security interests of the Soviet Union in the Baltic area. Could not a similar accommodation have been achieved without the bloodshed?

If we believe with Heracleitus that »all is flux, nothing is stationary», that history is an ever-flowing stream, then we can never step into the same water a second time. Yet speculating about what might have happened often helps us to understand what did happen.

One reason why giving in to Stalin's demands in 1939 could hardly have saved Finland from war was the nature of German policy. Hitler would not have respected Finnish neutrality in 1941, any more than he respected Swedish neutrality which he violated by blackmailing the Swedish government into allowing

German troops to march through Sweden into Finland. One way or another Finland would have been drawn into the conflict, not as an autonomous actor, but as a battlefield in the conflict between two big powers, without much chance to influence her own fate. After the Second World War the geopolitical situation was fundamentally different. Soviet security interests in the Baltic area were no longer directly threatened by a hostile power. The Finnish-Soviet accommodation reached in the late 1940's was never challenged by the West. Moscow could afford to take a more relaxed view of Finland.

Another question is whether Stalin would have been satisfied with what he asked for in November 1939. Here we enter the shadowy area of Soviet motives and intentions. Obviously these vary with opportunities and capabilities. Stalin himself said to the Finnish negotiators in November 1939 that his demands represented the minimum necessary to ensure the security of the Soviet Union: »My military advisers would like me to ask for much more.» Once war had started the minimum demands were superseded by the maximum objective embodied in the Kuusinen government. It is not unreasonable to assume that it was Stalin's ambition to recover for the Soviet Union all the territories that had been lost by Russia in the First World War. In the case of the Baltic states he also moved from minimum to maximum. In the autumn of 1939 he was content with military bases, in the summer of 1940 the three small states were incorporated into the Soviet Union.

But the Finns fought, and this seems to have made a profound impression on Stalin. Military prowess was probably the quality he admired most. He respected military power and nothing else, as was shown by his famous question about the Pope's divisions. He had probably thought that the Finnish divisions did not amount to much. But the Finnish resistance made him revise his plans. Kuusinen disappeared and was not brought out again in 1944. During a discussion on Finland at the Teheran Conference in December 1943, Stalin told Roosevelt and Churchill, as recorded by Charles Bohlen, that »any country that fought with such courage for its independence deserved consideration». After the war he went out of his way on several occasions to pay tribute to the skill and courage of Finnish soldiers. Finland in his eyes had passed a crucial test of manhood.

Such a Darwinian interpretation of history is no doubt repulsive to the rational mind, but that is not sufficient ground for dismissing it. The Winter War is not the only case in point. The Hungarians fought in 1956 against impossible odds and were duly crushed, but today Hungary enjoys a greater degree of national independence than Czechoslovakia which in 1938 and again in 1968 acted more rationally by submitting to superior force.

The way Stalin's mind worked was revealed by his conversation with Tito in April 1945, as reported by Milovan Djilas. »This war is not as in the past,» Stalin said at one point. »Whoever occupies a territory also imposes on it its social system. Everyone imposes his own system as far as his army can reach.» Just as Czar Nicholas I had remarked in 1850: »Where the Russian flag has once been hoisted it must not be lowered.»

The Russian flag was not hoisted in Finland. Finland remained free. True, the Finns had no more than marginal control over the external circumstances of their country during the Second World War. Their freedom of choice more often than not was freedom to choose between the bad and the worse. But ultimately it was their own decisions, not decisions imposed by others, that determined their fate. Just as when shooting a rapid one must keep rowing in order to steer, however futile or even absurd that may seem to someone watching from the shore, so did the Finns keep control over their own affairs, even at times when the current of events seemed irresistible. And they were prudent enough not to attempt to steer upstream, at least not for too long.

VI
The Shadow of Yalta

The continuing debate on the meaning of Yalta — a symbol of duplicity and betrayal for one side, security and stability for the other — hardly ever touches on the one country where the principles agreed upon by the Big Three in February 1945 have actually been carried out. The agreement was that the Soviet Union was entitled to make sure neighbouring countries would be run by »friendly governments» — friendly in the sense of respecting Soviet security — but that these governments must be freely elected by the peoples themselves. The only country in which such a marriage between the interests of Soviet security and parliamentary democracy was consummated was Finland where »free and unfettered elections», as prescribed at Yalta, were held within a month of the Big Three Conference, at a time when Hitler was still directing operations from his bunker in Berlin and Finnish troops were still driving the Germans out of Lapland: the first elections to be held in war-torn Europe.

The reason why this was possible in Finland was not because it was so decreed in Yalta. Finland was hardly even mentioned there. »Free and unfettered elections» were prescribed specifically for Poland.

Why could not Poland be more like Finland? After forty years the question still lingers on. Thus, for instance, Zbigniew Brzezinski in »Game Plan»: »The issue for the Soviet Union is whether to accept eventually a Poland that is more like Finland or to insist on continued ideological- political subordination.»

In Moscow's view the differences between Finland and Poland are of course profound. They go far back in history, as has been pointed out in a previous chapter. Strategically, Finland is peripheral, Poland pivotal. West of Finland lies neutral Sweden; west of Poland, Germany. At the Yalta Conference Stalin described Poland as a corridor through which the Germans had attacked Russia twice in thirty years. Today Poland is a corridor linking the Soviet Union with its bastion in Eastern Germany.

There is, however, another important difference which arises from the political and social conditions of the two countries themselves.

The political structure of post-war Finland was not hammered together in a deal between the victorious powers, to be imposed upon the country from the outside. Finland emerged from the war with its political system intact, without an army of occupation on its soil. Free and unfettered elections were an integral part of the Finnish system. The decision to resume the normal electoral process which had been interrupted by the war was taken several months before the Yalta Conference. It was not dictated by the Big Three.

Poland presents a sharp contrast. Her social fabric had been torn to shreds by five years of German occupation, and a new political system had to be constructed under the guns of the Red Army. The attempt made by Churchill and Roosevelt at the Yalta Conference to create a Poland in the image of their own societies was doomed to fail: liberal parliamentary democracy had no roots in Poland.

The same is true of the other countries of Eastern and Central Europe that had been occupied by Soviet forces, with the one exception of Czechoslovakia where in fact free elections were held in May 1946. In all the others various types of totalitarian regimes had been in power in the period before the Second World War. Poland had been run by Marshal Pilsudski and his colonels; Hungary by Admiral Horthy; Romania by the dictator Antonescu. None of these countries had had much practice with holding free and unfettered elections.

Totalitarianism of different shades held sway over the greater part of the Continent of Europe – in the Baltic states and in the Balkans, in Italy and Germany, in Spain and Portugal. Even in France parliamentary democracy was hard pressed.

Finland, too, had been touched by the totalitarian virus in the 1920's and early 1930s. After the Civil War of 1918 tension between Right and Left persisted. The militant nationalism of the young Republic expressed itself in intense anti-Communism. Agitation for the liberation of the Finnish-speaking people of Soviet Karelia was popular among university students. An extreme right-wing party with fascist trappings – the Patriotic People's Movement – campaigned for an authoritarian system of government to replace ineffectual parliamentarism. In 1930 the Communist party, which at the time held 23 seats out of 200 in Parliament, was declared illegal and membership of it treason. It was a time of Finnish McCarthyism.

Yet, in spite of Finland's traditional ties with Germany, support for Nazism was confined to the lunatic fringe. In 1932 an inept attempt by a group of right-wing extremists to stage a coup d'etat was suppressed without bloodshed. Isolated acts of political violence that occurred in the early part of the 1930s turned conservative opinion against the militant Right. Support for the Patriotic People's Movement dwindled from 14 seats in 1930 to eight in 1939.

By the end of the 1930s it was clear that democracy had won in Finland. This was acknowledged by the German ambassador in Helsinki who in May 1938 advised Berlin not to expect ideological conquests »among a nation 90 % of which is democratic and 40 % socialist». In 1937, the Social- Democratic party joined the Agrarian and Liberal parties in a government coalition straddling the dividing line between Right and Left: an act of national reconciliation that enabled the Finnish people to close ranks before the coming storm.

The Finnish system of government not only withstood the challenge of right-wing totalitarianism in the 1930s, it also survived the wartime association with Nazi Germany, and it has functioned virtually unchanged through the economic and social upheavals that have taken place since the Second World War. Indeed, it is today among the oldest systems of government in operation. Very few states in the world can match Finland's record of political continuity.

Obviously one reason for this is that Finland has not been conquered by a foreign power. But this does not explain why her system of government has not been affected by internal change, as was the Swedish system in the 1970s. The answer may be found in its construction which in important respects differs from the classical parliamentary model.

The basic elements of constitutional government date from the time Finland was part of the Kingdom of Sweden: the equality of citizens before the law, the independence of the judiciary, local self-rule, and an efficient and uncorrupt civil service have a tradition of many centuries. Many of the central state institutions date from the latter half of the 19th century. But parliamentary democracy in the modern sense has its origin in the reform carried out in 1906, when the old Diet of Four Estates was replaced by a unicameral parliament (Eduskunta) of 200 members elected by all Finns over the age of 24 (now 18) on the basis of proportional representation, and at the same time legislation guaranteeing freedom of speech, assembly and association was enacted. Thus Finland almost overnight was transformed into one of the most advanced democracies of the world – the first country in Europe to grant women the vote. (Outside Europe only New Zealand had done so earlier.)

The parliamentary reform in Finland had been approved by Emperor Nicholas II at a moment when the Czarist regime had been weakened by defeat in war and unrest at home. But Russian policy soon reverted to oppression. The new Finnish legislature was reduced to an empty shell. Such laws as it managed to pass were vetoed by the Emperor. The great hopes raised by the new electoral system among the growing workers' movement – movingly expressed in Aulis Sallinen's opera »The Red Line» – were frustrated. The Social- Democratic Party, which had emerged as a powerful political force with nearly 100 000 members and eighty seats in the first Parliament elected in 1907, began to lose faith in reform through the ballot. The stage was set for the tragedy of 1918: a civil war that for one side was part of the revolutionary class struggle, for the other a war of liberation from Russian rule.

Around 100 000 men fought on the Red side, against 70 000 on the White. Some seven thousand men were killed in battle, but almost three times as many were murdered or executed by both sides or died later in prison camps. The savage struggle left deep scars in Finnish society. Much of what happened in the first fifty years since the birth of the Republic can be explained as a reaction to 1918. It not only left a sense of bitter hostility among the defeated part the population; it also made restoration and maintenance of national unity the overriding issue in Finnish politics: Still today the phrase »Never again» means »Never again a divided nation».

One of the lessons drawn from the experiences of the civil war was that Finland needed a strong head of state who would stand above party division. The conservatives who had emerged as victors in 1918 believed that only a monarchy could ensure stability and order. As one of their leaders J.K. Paasikivi explained, in a small country all know each other too well, none could gain the respect needed by a head of state. So a king had to be imported from abroad. Since Sweden had failed to support the Finnish war of liberation, the Swedish royal house was ruled out. The only solid bulwark against the spread of revolution and chaos seemed to be the Kaiser's Germany, whose armies at the end of 1917, and indeed far into 1918, were undisputed masters of Eastern Europe. Finland's future therefore was to be anchored to German support. The election of a German prince as king of Finland was to ensure that Germany would continue to protect Finnish independence. The man chosen was Prince Friedrich Karl of Hessen, a nephew of the Kaiser.

This bizarre episode came to an end with the capitulation of Germany in November 1918 and the collapse of the German monarchy. By that time Finland had become compromised in Western eyes, and a complete turnabout in Finnish policy was demanded by the victorious Allies as a condition for recognition of Finnish independence. The German King-elect abdicated in December 1918 before setting foot on Finnish soil. The pro-German political leaders, including Paasikivi, stood aside, and in the first parliamentary elections in the beginning of 1919 the republicans gained a large majority.

Nevertheless, at the insistence of conservative

opinion, the republican constitution adopted in 1919 laid strong emphasis on executive power in the person of the president: a Gaullist concept thirty years before General de Gaulle. The president, elected for six years by an electoral college of 301 members chosen by proportional representation, directs foreign policy and is commander-in- chief of the defence forces. He appoints the prime minister and the other members of the cabinet, who must enjoy the confidence of Parliament: a provision that makes the government, though not the president himself, responsible to the legislature. The president presides over cabinet meetings, and he may even overrule his ministers, though this has happened very rarely. He also has the right to dissolve parliament and order new elections: a power exercised only in exceptional circumstances. The president presents bills to Parliament, ratifies laws and issues decrees, and appoints top civil servants, military officers and judges.

One of the ironies of Finnish history is that had the monarchy prevailed, it surely would have been reduced to political impotence, as has happened in the other Scnadinavian countries, and the monarch would now be a mere figurehead, useful perhaps for tourism and export promotion, whereas the compromise of 1919 has provided Finland with powerful political leadership, including that of Paasikivi, who as president in 1946 to 1956 had no difficulty in gaining and maintaining the respect of his countrymen.

The presidency as an institution has indeed a cardinal importance in Finnish national life. It has carried forward the ancient tradition of loyalty to the Sovereign into the modern age in which the sovereign is the nation itself. Unlike his American or French counterpart, the Finnish president, once elected, must cease to act as the leader of his party. He stands above the parliamentary battle, and public criticism of his person tends to be muted. The ceremonies and rituals surrounding the president reflect and maintain the deep-rooted reverence of the Finnish people toward their head of state. To sense this one only has to observe the public on an official occasion as it rises in respectful silence to greet the president whose entry is heralded by the strains of a military march celebrating the heroic deeds of Finnish troops in the Thirty Year War.

Those who believe that political institutions determine political behaviour can find a great deal of supporting evidence in the Finnish experience. In times of crisis and danger each of the Finnish presidents, in spite of great differences in background, personality and political outlook, has played the leading role written for him in the Constitution. The precidency has above all ensured continuity and consistency in foreign policy, qualities that often are damaged in the parliamentary battles.

The influence of institutional design on political behaviour can be traced even more clearly in parliamentary politics.

The Finnish system is unique among European parliamentary democracies in two important respects. One is the use of qualified majorities; the other, the way private property rights are protected against government intervention. In practical terms, one third of the votes in Parliament – 67 out of 200 – can block any legislation, except for budget laws that remain in force for one year only. An even smaller minority, one sixth, can prevent the passing of laws that abridge the rights of private ownership. This applies not only to nationalisation but also to such measures of regulation as price controls.

It could not happen in Finland, as has happened in Britain and France, that parliament first decides by a narrow majority to nationalize an industry and then after a new election by an equally narrow majority decides to denationalize it. It could not happen in Finland because nationalisation would require a two-third's majority — a level of support well beyond the reach of the parties of the Left which only twice in seventy years have managed to gain a simple majority of parliamentary seats. In fact no nationalization on ideological ground has been carried out in Finland. Such public ownership as does exist has come about for reasons unrelated to socialist doctrine.

The requirement of qualified majorities acts like a built-in stabilizer preventing sudden swings between Right and Left in government policy. Structural changes in the economy or society can be carried out only on the basis of wide agreement between the major parties. The system is designed to defuse confrontations, to reward moderation and discourage extremism. It induces politicians to seek consensus and build coalitions across the dividing line between Right and Left, as happened in 1937 between the parties that less than twenty years earlier had fought each other in a murderous civil war.

VII
The Communist Challenge

Thus Finland in 1945 was very different from Poland. But how was Finland different from Czechoslovakia, a country with a strong democratic tradition which none-theless was taken over by the Communists after the Second World War?

In the first years after the end of the war political developments in Finland and Czechoslovakia did seem to run along parallel lines. In both countries the Com-munist party gained strong support in the first post-war elections. In Finland, the Communists together with a small group of left- wing Socialists allied with them received 23,5 per cent of the votes and 49 seats out of 200 in Parliament. The Communists, the Social-Democrats and the Agrarian party, all three being roughly equal in strength, formed a coalition govern-ment which, like its counterparts in France and Italy as well as in the countries of Eastern and Central Eu-rope, mirrored the Grand Alliance that had won the war and was expected to run the post-war world.

The Communists could claim that their cause had been vindicated by events: They now represented the winning side in the struggle against Fascism − the wave of the future. They demanded a complete reorien-tation of Finnish policy, not only in foreign relations but also in economic and social terms, and the removal from public life of those who were responsible for the policy that had led to war and defeat. They insisted on obtaining the post of Minister of the Interior for their own man, and he used his power to appoint Communists to key positions in the police forces. Many Finns feared their civil liberties were in danger.

At this dark moment in their country's history the Finnish people, in what must seem to an outsider an almost perverse defiance of the demands for change, turned for leadership to two old men who appeared to personify the past: Marshal Mannerheim, the former Czarist officer, who to the end of his days persisted in using the term Bolshevik to describe the Soviet leaders; and the former monarchist Juho Kusti Paasikivi, a retired banker who had been the chairman of the Conservatives − a party then confined to impotent opposition. But precisely because they were men of the past, they could reassure the nation that the change that was inevitable could be contained within the established frame of Finnish freedom and democracy.

Mannerheim's unassailable personal authority ensured national unity at the critical moment in September 1944, when the armed forces, still unbeaten in the field, had to withdraw behind the border agreed upon in the armistice talks and turn against their former comrades-in-arms, the Germans in the North. Under his leadership the transition from war to peace was made without internal disruption. But in April 1946 the 79-year-old Marshal, whose health was failing, retired, and Paasikivi was virtually unanimously elected president for the remainder of Mannerheim's term. In 1950 he was re-elected, at the age of 80, for a full term of six years.

Paasikivi brought to his office a life-time's experience of dealing with the problem of reconciling Finnish national aspirations with Russian interests. He had began his political career in the early years of the century, at the time when the autonomy of Finland was facing the challenge of Czarist repression. He had then joined the group of conservative politicians who had been convinced that the essential national interests of the Finnish people, above all their cultural identity, could be preserved only through prudent appeasement of the strategic interests and prestige of the Russian empire. This conviction never left him. In 1920 he was chosen to negotiate the first peace treaty between independent Finland and the Soviet Union and he was successful in obtaining Soviet recognition of Finland's historic frontiers; too successful, as he later was to point out, in that these frontiers almost touched the suburbs of Leningrad, thus creating a sense of insecurity in the minds of the Soviet leaders. In October 1939 Paasikivi was chosen to lead the Finnish delegation that had to face Stalin's demands, and after the Winter War he served as Finland's Minister to Moscow, where he gained the respect and trust of Stalin and Molotov as a man who, in spite of his opposition to Communism, genuinely sought an accommodation between his country and the Soviet Union.

With the approach of the German-Soviet clash Paasikivi found himself increasingly out of tune with the spirit prevailing in Helsinki, and he resigned a few weeks before Finland once again was embroiled in war with the Soviet Union. Throughout the war years he stayed out of office, and so, in 1944, was untainted by association with Nazi Germany. As he himself later noted, a small nation like Finland always needs, not an opposition shadow cabinet, but a reserve team ready to step into office whenever a turn of the great wheel of world politics makes a change of leadership necessary. In 1919, the turn of the wheel had thrown Paasikivi out of office; in 1944, it brought him back.

Although the outcome of the war had in effect confirmed Finland's existence as an independent state, the foundations of her security seemed to have been destroyed. Finnish policy had been based on the assumption that the Soviet Union, combining traditional Russian imperialism with the Communist doctrine of world conquest, inevitably must aim at destroying Finnish independence. If this assumption was valid there was no hope for Finland. The balance of power in Europe had changed, irrevocably as it then seemed. Germany was in ruins. The Western powers were allied with the Soviet Union; neither their interests nor their influence extended to the Eastern shores of the Baltic. Indeed, American policy at the end of the Second World War was to warn Finland not to expect any kind of support against the Soviet Union. Finland was alone, exposed to the overwhelming force of the Soviet Union. Not surprisingly the Finnish General Staff, without informing the political leaders, began to store arms into secret caches in preparation for a last act of guerilla war that seemed inevitable.

In this situation Paasikivi offered a new concept of Finnish-Soviet relations that not only was tailored to fit the prevailing strategic realities but also was designed to restore the faith of the Finnish people in an independent future. He had always argued that the Russian interest in Finland was primarily strategic and defensive. It was to make sure that the city Peter the Great had built would be safe from an attack through Finland. This, according to Paasikivi, was a »legitimate interest», a subtle phrase in the spirit of Yalta, which conveyed both the direction and the limit of his policy of appeasement. It was designed to assure the Soviet government that its need for security would be satisfied, while serving notice that Finland would not yield to demands going beyond the legitimate – ideological demands for instance. By convincing the Soviet leaders that Finland in no circumstances would turn against them, Pasikivi believed the Finns could secure their own independence and way of life. He thus undertook a double task of persuasion: first, to make the Kremlin trust an independent Finland, and second, to make the Finnish people bend themselves to the facts of power and work together to achieve the first objective.

And the Finnish people did work hard, in those first years after the end of the war, to convince theSoviet leaders that Finland could be trusted to keep her word. Fullfillment of the terms of the Armistice Agreement (and later the Peace Treaty of 1947) was given priority over all other tasks. The goods demanded by the Soviet Union as a war indemnity were delivered punctually on schedule: Finland is probably the only country in modern history that has voluntarily paid its war reparations in full. Another unique achievement was the resettlement of the Karelian people, one tenth of the total population, within six to eight years, a process that removed a potentially explosive issue from the Finnish-Soviet agenda.

This was accomplished without any foreign assistance, for in 1947 the Finnish government reluctantly decided to decline the invitation to join the Marshall Plan so as to avoid arousing Soviet suspicions. It was a decision that cost the country many millions of dollars, but probably did more than anything else to reinforce the credibility of Paasikivi's policy in the eyes of the Soviet leaders. The Marshall Plan was designed to save Europe from Communism, but Finland may have saved herself from Communism by saying no to the Marshall Plan.

A less tangible, but in a sense an even more painful act of appeasement was the trial and conviction of eight leading politicians held responsible for Finland's entry into the war against the Soviet Union. This was done in 1946 under a special retroactive law, a procedure that ran contrary to the fundamental concepts of justice prevailing in Finland, and was as repugnant to the judges as it was to the accused. Both sides played their role in the trial in the spirit of national service, acting in the belief that such a sacrifice of principle was part of the price Finland had to pay in order to retain control of her own affairs. If anyone had to be punished for Finland's wartime policies it was better that this be done by Finland herself — the only one of all European countries engaged in the Second World War in which the transition from war to peace was carried out without a single execution. The eight men accused of responsibility for Finland's wartime policy were sentenced to prison terms ranging from two to ten years, and all were released after serving half their term. In the eyes of the majority of the people they were never dishonoured. When former President Risto Ryti, who had received the longest sentence of ten years, died in 1956, he was given a state funeral, at which his successor, President Urho Kekkonen, spoke of his selfless service to his country. Former Prime Minister Edwin Linkomies, a professor of Latin and Greek, became rector of Helsinki University, and the Social-Democratic leader, Väinö Tanner, returned to Parliament and in 1957 was re-elected chairman of his party.

There can be no doubt that the Finnish performance, perhaps especially the prompt deliveries of the reparations, impressed the men in the Kremlin. But in the West, Paasikivi's faith in a policy of seeking salvation through good works was rejected as naive. As the wartime alliance was coming apart, perceptions of Soviet policy were rapidly changed. According to conventional wisdom the Soviet Union was an aggressive, expansionist power which, far from being in need of security itself, was bent upon imposing Communist rule throughout Europe, by subversion if possible, by military conquest if necessary. Ernest Bevin, the British Foreign Secretary, warned his Cabinet in 1948 that Moscow was »planning physical control of the Eurasian land mass and eventual control of the world: no less a thing than that». Such a power could not be appeased, it could only be contained by force. True, Finland had not been turned into a Communist satellite, an awkward fact for people with tidy minds. But surely sooner or later, sooner rather than later, this oversight would be put right.

Early in 1948 that moment seemed to have arrived. On February 23 President Paasikivi received a personal letter from Generalissimus Stalin. It was short and to the point. Finland, Stalin pointed out, was the only one of the European neighbours of the Soviet Union with which it had not yet made a defence agreement against a recurrence of German aggression. He wished to know whether Finland were prepared to conclude with the Soviet Union a treaty of mutual assistance similar to the treaties the Soviet Union had shortly earlier concluded with Hungary and Romania.

The date of the letter was significant. February 23 was the day on which the Communist bid for power in Czechoslovakia was reaching its climax. Western opinion was in a state of shock. When Stalin's letter to Paasikivi was made public a few days later, it became immediately linked in the minds of Western observers with the Communist coup d'etat in Prague. The two events were regarded as a concerted advance of international Communism upon the remnants of Western democracy in the Soviet sphere of influence. The interests of the Soviet state and of the international Communist movement were seen to fuse into a vast conspiracy moving with perfect precision and coordination towards its goal of world domination.

Stalin's stated purpose of creating a defence against

future German aggression was dismissed as an obvious pretext. Germany, divided, occupied and disarmed, was in ruins: what was there to fear? The real purpose of the proposed treaty with Finland, it was believed, was to provide a legal excuse for establishing military bases or moving troops into Finland, not in order to repell a German aggression but to destroy Finnish democracy. It was taken for granted that the Finns had no choice but to submit. Stalin's letter was regarded not as a proposal for negociations but as a command to be obeyed. Finland as an independent state was speedily written off in the West. The Western powers would do nothing to save Finland; but they could begin to organize themselves to defend a line west of Finland.

From Moscow, the European scene looked different. In the Soviet view, the Marshall Plan was primarily a means of restoring the strength of Germany as a spearhead of an anti- Soviet coalition. Having twice in a lifetime seen the Russian state come close to destruction through German aggression, the Soviet leaders were obsessed with the danger of a resurrection of German power. Stalin had learned from history to look beyond the ruins of today. Throughout the 1930s Soviet diplomacy had laboured in vain to induce Russia's western neighbours to agree to security arrangements against Germany, and the lessons of the war had only confirmed, in Soviet eyes, the need for such arrangements. During the war years, mutual assistance pact had been concluded with Czechoslovakia and Poland. In February 1948 similar pacts were signed with Hungary and Romania. Bulgaria was to follow in March.

As for Finland, the Soviet wish for a defence pact had been discussed for the first time in the secret Soviet- Finnish talks in 1938-39. During the war the Soviet government had asked the British as early as

4

The statue of Emperor Alexander II, Grand Duke of Finland (1818–1881), in the center of Helsinki. (Lehtikuva)

Carl Gustaf Mannerheim, (1867–1951), Marshal of Finland, President in 1944–46. (Otava)

Juho Kusti Paasikivi, (1870–1956), President in 1946–56. (Otava)

Mauno Henrik Koivisto, b. 1923, was elected President in 1982 for six years and is the leading candidate for re-election in 1988. (Press-foto)

Urho Kaleva Kekkonen, (1900–1986), President in 1956–81. (Otava)

Finlandia Hall, a conference and concert center designed by Alvar Aalto, the scene of the signing of the Final Act of the Conference on European Security and Cooperation in August 1975. (Pressfoto)

President Kekkonen on a hunting trip with Soviet leader Nikita Chruchev in December 1963. (Yhtyneiden Kuvalehtien kuva-arkisto)

1942 to give advance approval of its plan to conclude a mutual defence treaty with Finland.

After the war, the first initiative for defence talks between Finland and the Soviet Union had been taken by Marshal Mannerheim in the beginning of 1945. As a former Russian general he had looked at Finland from the other side of the hill. He believed his country's independence could be strengthened if it could be shown that Finland was prepared to serve the defensive needs of her neighbour. Moscow did not respond at the time, presumably because Finland's status had not yet been confirmed by a peace treaty, but soon after this had been done the Soviet government took up the issue of a defence pact with Finland, first during a visit of a Finnish delegation to Moscow in November 1947, then more formally in Stalin's letter to Paasikivi.

To President Paasikivi, the idea of a treaty with the Soviet Union was not unacceptable in itself. Indeed, the logic of his own policy impelled him to agree to an arrangement that would satisfy the »legitimate security interests» of the Soviet Union. But the models offered by Stalin he found wholly unacceptable. The Soviet treaties with Hungary and Romania imposed on the parties an unlimited obligation to political consultations in time of peace and automatic mutual assistance in the event of war. Such a treaty would have made Finland an ally of the Soviet in any and all conflicts between East and West. An overwhelming majority of the Finnish people were totally opposed to an alliance with the Soviet Union − or with any other major power: For if there is one dominant theme in Finland's foreign policy, it is the desire to avoid being drawn into the conflicts and controvercies between more powerful nations. Paasikivi thus had to try to persuade Stalin to be content with an arrangement that, while satisfying Soviet security requierements, would enable Finland to stay outside the two opposing military alliances which were taking shape in Europe.

The Finnish president moved with majestic deliberation. Before making public Stalin's letter he informed the government and the chairmen of the parliamentary groups. This took five days. On February 27 he sent Stalin a brief acknowledgement pointing out that in Finland a treaty with a foreign power needed parliamentary approval and therefore the representatives of the people had to be consulted. On March 5 he received the written views of the parliamentary groups. It took him another four days to appoint a delegation for the negotiations with the Soviet Union. On March 9 he replied to Stalin suggesting that the negotiations be held in Moscow. Another nine days passed before the instructions to the Finnish negotiators had been drawn up and approved by the president. On March 20 most members of the delegation travelled to Moscow by train, and its head, Prime Minister Mauno Pekkala, left four days later by plane. On March 25, more than a month after receipt of Stalin's letter, the first meeting between representatives of Finland and the Soviet Union took place in Moscow.

The timetable of the Finnish preparations was eloquent in itself. It was an assertion of Finnish independence and a demonstration of the democratic process. The Finnish people were being reassured: their interests were not going to be signed away by frightened men in hasty and secret deals. The president himself stayed in the capital so as not to commit his prestige in advance. Parliament was fully consulted, not only before the negociations but also at each subsequent stage. As Paasikivi put it, it was better to fail to reach an agreement in Moscow than to sign a treaty that would be rejected by Parliament.

But the elaborate process of consultations also served another purpose. It fully displayed the strong opposition that existed in Finland to any kind of a defence treaty. Of the three parties represented in the coalition government then in power, only the Communists were prepared to support the kind of treaty Stalin had proposed; the Social-Democrats and the Agrarian party both declared their opposition to a treaty containing military clauses that might involve the country in international conflicts. Opinion among the opposition parties was against even entering negotiations with Moscow.

As the Finnish delegation left Helsinki, rumours of an impending Communist attempt to seize power began to circulate. The stage seemed to be set for a double squeeze − external pressure combined with internal subversion − to put an end to the independence of Finland. Once again, as in the beginning of the century, the cry was »Finis Finlandiae».

VIII
Paasikivi's Triumph

After all the alarms and anxieties the encounter in Moscow was an anticlimax. The Soviet leaders readily agreed to set aside the models suggested in Stalin's letter and asked the Finns to put forward their own suggestions. The Finnish draft was then accepted as basis for negotiations, and the final text conformed in all essentials to Paasikivi's concept of Finland's role as Russia's neighbour.

An episode at the Kremlin banquet celebrating the signing of the treaty on April 6, 1948, revealed the sense of relief felt by the Finnish negotiators. Stalin as host spoke of the compromise reached in the talks. »What compromise?» interrupted one of the Finns. »The treaty was dictated by Paasikivi.» After a moment of stunned silence, Stalin burst out laughing. The Finn who spoke was Urho Kekkonen, the man who a few years later was to succeed Paasikivi as president.

The treaty is unique among the scores of security arrangements made between the big powers and smaller states in the period after the Second World War. Its first article states that »should either Finland, or the Soviet Union through the territory of Finland, become the object of military aggression on the part of Germany or any power allied with Germany, Finland will, true to its duty as a sovereign state, fight to repell aggression». Finnish forces would be acting only within the limits of Finland's own boundaries. The Soviet Union would extend to Finland assistance »if necessary» and »as mutually agreed between the parties»: this meant,as interpreted by the Finnish Parliament, that any agreement on military assistance or military cooperation with the Soviet Union would constitute an independent treaty which would have to be judged on its merits with regard to possible parliamentary approval.

Commenting on the treaty in a broadcast speech to the Finnish people on April 9, 1948, Paasikivi pointed out that the first article really was a statement of the obvious: it described what in any case would happen in the event of an attack against Finland. The obligation to hold consultations between the two parties was narrowed down to cases where a threat of the kind of military aggression described in the first article had been found to exist. And according to Paasikivi, both countries had to agree that there was such a threat.

The treaty thus lacked the essential characteristics of a treaty of alliance, such as regular consultations in time of peace and automatic mutual assistance in case of war. It had been drafted, as was stated in the preamble, »taking into account Finland's desire to stay outside the conflicts of interests between the great powers» — that is, Finland's neutrality. Accordingly, Paasikivi was able to state in his commentary that »Finland had in principle the right to stay neutral in a war between other states».

At the time Finland's aspirations to neutrality were still severely handicapped. As the president himself put it, the lease of the Porkkala military base held by the Soviet Union by virtue of the Peace Treaty, as well as its right of free transit through Finnish territory to and from Porkkala, »lent Finnish neutrality a colour of its own which did not quite fit the handbooks of international law». But as a clue to future policies the neutrality clause in the preamble of the treaty had a vital importance.

Why did the Soviet government so readily accept the Finnish draft for the treaty? One explanation that suggests itself is that, once again, the time gained by Paasikivi's slow tempo had strengthened the Finnish position. In the four weeks that had elapsed between Stalin's letter and the beginning of the talks in Moscow the world had changed. The Western powers, shocked into action by the events in Czechoslovakia, had taken a long step toward organizing their common defence. NATO was being conceived. In the North, Norway was about to abandon its traditional neutrality; even in Sweden defence measures were intensified. At the same time, though this was not then known to outsiders, Stalin's quarrel with Tito was coming to a head. The Soviet leaders could hardly have wished to take on more trouble.

But there could be a simpler explanation. The Finnish- Soviet treaty resembled closely the proposals made by the Soviet government exactly ten years earlier. It represented a long-term objective of the Soviet Union. After the experiences of the Winter War Stalin probably did not expect to get more out of Finland in 1948 than what he had proposed in 1938. He knew well that anything beyond what was finally agreed would have met with strong resistance. On the eve of the departure of the Finnish delegation from Moscow, Molotov anxiously enquired whether he could be sure that the treaty as signed would actually be ratified by the Finnish Parliament.

The treaty was ratified on April 28, by 157 votes against 11, with 30 absent, but the debate preceding the vote clearly revealed the reluctance and misgivings of many members. It also echoed the internal tension then prevailing in Finland. The rumours of a Communist plan to seize power had prompted the president to order preventive measures. Troops were standing by, the police were alerted, and a gunboat was anchored in Helsinki harbour opposite the presidential residence.

No coup d'etat was in fact attempted, and we shall never know with certainty whether this was because of the precautions taken or because no coup had ever been planned. Later research has revealed that the Finnish Communist party at the time was far from being the formidable force it was generally supposed to be. Its leadership was divided, and the signals it received from Moscow were often mixed and obscure. The fact remains, however, that most people in Finland believed at the time that the Communists did plan to take over power and that they had been forestalled by Paasikivi's resolute action. And this belief had a profound effect on political developments. In May, the communist minister of the interior received a vote of no-confidence in Parliament and was dismissed by the president. In July, the Communist party suffered a heavy defeat in parliamentary elections and was left out of the government. Once again, internal developments in Finland mirrored the state of international relations: the Grand Alliance had broken up, the Cold War had begun.

Moscow showed its displeasure in several ways. Soviet media echoed the anguished cries of the Finnish Communists and their attacks against Paasikivi himself. In the winter of 1949-50 Finnish-Soviet trade talks were stalled without explanation. Just before the presidential election in January 1950 the Soviet government accused Finland of harbouring war criminals. But Soviet reactions were carefully kept within the range of what could be described as correct relations between the countries. Moscow made no demands, no threats. In spring 1950, after the re-election of Paasikivi and the appointment of Urho Kekkonen as Prime Minister, a trade agreement was signed, although the Communists were kept out of the government. The interests of the Soviet state clearly were given precedence over ideological aspirations.

The difference between Finland and Czechoslovakia in 1948 is revealed by a comparison between internal conditions in the two countries. Communism was stronger in Czechoslovakia than in Finland. The Czech party had the support of 40 per cent of the voters, the Finnish party 23 per cent. In Czechoslovakia, Communists held important positions in the civil service and armed forces, in Finland they had hardly any influence at all in the central organs of government. Attitudes to Russia also differed: the Czechs and Slovaks on the whole looked upon the Soviet Union as a friend and ally, the only power that in 1938 had declared its readiness to come to the aid of Czechoslovakia, while most Finns still considered the Soviet Union their arch enemy. Finally, President Paasikivi made it clear he was prepared to take strong action against the Communists; President Beneš gave in to the Communist demands without resistance.

In Czechoslovakia the Communists were strong enough to seize power by their own efforts; in Finland only a massive Soviet intervention by military force could have overthrown the elected government. At no point did Moscow encourage the Finnish Communists to expect such an intervention. Indeed, there is every indication that Stalin was satisfied with the relationship between Finland and the Soviet Union as it had been defined by Paasikivi. When he had told Tito that as a result of the Second World War both the Soviet Union and the Western Allies would extend their system of government so far as their armies would reach, he had not added »but no further», but such a rider appears to have guided his actions. He did not move against Tito and he did not move against Finland. He did not have to move against Czechoslovakia.

On the last day of 1948 Paasikivi noted in his diary: »The Communists coup in Prague was the most important event of the past year. It opened the eyes of the world. . .» For Paasikivi himself, 1948 had been a year of triumph. He had been able to demonstrate in action that the »legitimate security interests» of the Soviet Union could be satisfied by Finland without giving in to the Communists at home.

IX
Toward Consensus

In the Western view the events of 1948 meant that Finland was out of the emergency ward but still on the critical list. The Communists, though out of office, continued to exercise considerable influence in political life. As in France and Italy, they maintained their parliamentary strength at above 20 per cent of the total vote. In the presidential election of 1956 they were able to play king- maker by helping Urho Kekkonen, the candidate of the Agrarian party, to defeat his Social-Democratic rival by the narrowest possible margin. In the labour unions the Communists were strong, though never dominant.

In the years of the Cold War every political skirmish in any European country was judged in terms of its possible effect on the strategic contest between two systems: Communism versus Capitalism, the Free World against the Captive Nations of the Sino-Soviet bloc, or as seen from the other side, the Camp of Peace against the Camp of Imperialism; either way, the Children of Light against the Children of Darkness. There could be no doubt about which side was making more progress in a material sense. Yet the West on the whole felt itself to be on the defensive, like an old champion grown soft and flabby facing a lean and tough opponent.

The launching of the world's first space satellite, the Sputnik, in October 1957, jolted the West into taking the Soviet challenge seriously. Soviet leader Nikita

Khrushchev's boast in 1960 that the Soviet Union would catch up and overtake the United States in industrial and farm production within twenty years was not seen to be as absurd as it actually turned out to be. »Your grandchildren will live under Communism!» Khrushchev shouted at Richard Nixon, then Vice-President, during their famous »kitchen debate» in 1959 in Moscow. The prediction touched a sensitive nerve in the West. An influential part of opinionmakers tended to use a double standard in judging the merits of the two competing systems - capitalism by its actual performance, communism by its promise of a better future.

The Western democracies suffered of a cronic lack of selfconfidence, and one of its symptoms was an over-anxious concern for the health of democracy in Finland. It sometimes expressed itself in grotesque fantasies, as for instance when in the late 1950s serious American commentators suggested the Finnish people might be converted to Communism because they were able to watch TV programs transmitted by Soviet stations across the Gulf of Finland. (In actual fact Finnish TV programs, including Dallas and Dynasty and enticing commercials, have an eager audience in Soviet Estonia.) President Kekkonen tried to reassure Western opinion by declaring in 1960 that even if all the rest of Europe were to go Communist, Finland would stick to her system of government. A sharp twist was added to this statement by the fact that it was made in the presence of Nikita Khrushchev who was visiting Helsinki. But the Soviet leader was not outwitted. In that case, he replied, Finland would be like an outdoor museum where the Soviets would send their young people to see what capitalism had been like.

The ideological issue did not remain so clearcut for long. By the mid-sixties the line of battle had become blurred. The improvement in the relations between United States and the Soviet Union – détente as it was later called – lessened the fear of war in Europe. At the same time, in the minds of many young Europeans, the American dream was distorted into a nightmare by the cruel war in Vietnam and racial strife and political violence in the United States itself. The New Left turned against all the traditional values of Western society. With memories of Stalin's terror fading, the Soviet Union appeared to many Europeans, and not only to those on the far Left, not as an aggressive expansionist power, but rather as the defender of peace and stability in Europe; a repressive society but less so than before; less prosperous then the West but slowly improving its standard of living in conditions of social security. Belief in an inevitable convergence between the two systems was gaining ground. It was encouraged by the communist parties in Western Europe which were beginning to break out of the Stalinist mould.

In Finland, manifestations of militant radicalism were relatively mild. But for the first time in Finnish history the Communist party in the 1960s began to attract young intellectuals, especially the sons and daughters of affluent families. (It was said at the time that the Finnish Communist party did not have to demand the nationalization of industry: they would inherit it.) Among the Social- Democrats, too, attitudes were changing. The Communists were no longer regarded as agents of a foreign power or advocates of violent revolution, but rather as potential partners in social reform. A majority among the Communists themselves were desperately anxious to prove themselves as good Finns and democrats.

In 1966, President Kekkonen decided to give them a chance to do so. After 18 years in opposition the Communist party was accepted as a partner in a coalition government with the Social- Democratic party and the Center party (formerly the Agrarian party). In a speech in February 1967 Kekkonen pointed out that, just as peaceful cooperation in international relations meant increasing cooperation between states with different social systems, it should be possible to cooperate internally with the Communists in a spirit of peaceful competition between different ideologies. Throughout his political career — he had been elected to Parliament for the first time in 1937 — Kekkonen had worked for national unity. He could not accept the view that every fifth voter must be regarded as unpatriotic. Treating the Communists as outcasts could only drive them further into hostility. The time had come, Kekkonen declared, »to integrate» the Communists into Finnish society. This could only be achieved by allowing them to take part in political life on an equal footing with the other parties.

Kekkonen at the time believed in convergence. He wrote in a letter in 1963: »I am neither a Hegelian nor a Marxist, but I do believe that the historical trend is towards a synthesis replacing the present struggle (between the two systems).» His analysis anticipated the emergence of the trend within the Communist movement which later became known as »Eurocommunism». But his opening to the Left was received with many misgivings in Finland and in the West. Few Western observers were prepared to share Kekkonen's assumption that the Communists would be ready to put national interest first and abide by the rules of the parliamentary game. Ominously, Moscow welcomed the entry of the Communists into the Finnish government. The Soviet line at the time was to encourage the Communist parties in Western Europe to break out of their isolation and join other »peaceloving forces» in a modern version of the Popular Front. This looked like a maneuver designed to undermine Western unity from within. Eurocommunism, in this view, was the Trojan horse by which the enemies of NATO would be smuggled into the governments of such countries as Italy or France; once inside, they would cling to power by any means. Western leaders had little faith in their own system.

What actually happened was something neither Kekkonen nor his critics had foreseen. Eurocommunism did begin to undermine the rigid structure of Europe, but on the Eastern side. The Prague Spring showed what convergence meant in practice: a movement in one direction only, away from the Soviet model. The occupation of Czechoslovakia by Warsaw Pact forces in the autumn of 1968 put an end for almost twenty years to all efforts to reform the Soviet system from within. It also uncovered the deep cracks that had developed in the very foundations of the international Communist movement.

In Finland, the Communist party was openly split between the dogmatists who believed the Soviet Union could do no wrong, and the reformists who insisted that every Communist party must have the right to follow its own road in accordance with national requirements. The latter were clearly in the majority, but the Soviet Union supported the minority faction: no number of votes could undo the sin of heresy. The problem for President Kekkonen turned out to be, not how to get the Communists out of government, but how to keep them in and make them share responsibility for unpopular economic policies.

Participation in a coalition government means making compromises, and compromise, by definition, is alien to a revolutionary party. The dogmatists feared, quite rightly, that continued cooperation with the other parties would ultimately lead to a loss of identity, making the Communist party a mere annex to Social Democracy. But the only alternative they could offer was withdrawal into sterile opposition. The dilemma facing the Communist party was insoluble: either way it was doomed to lose influence and support. In 1981, the party finally withdrew from the government.

The policy of selfdestruction pursued by the Finnish Communist party in the 1970s was carefully noted by François Mitterrand, the French Socialist leader, who after his victory in the presidential election of 1979 effectively used the Finnish recipe to divide and weaken the French Communist party.

The primary cause of the decline of Communism in Finland was of course social change. The party had drawn most of its support from two groups: industrial workers, especially in heavy industry, and poor farmers with small holdings in the outlying areas of eastern and northern Finland who voted Communist as a protest against their condition rather than out of any Marxist conviction. By the beginning of the 1970s, the number of industrial workers had already passed its peak, while the Communist strongholds in the rural areas were being rapidly depopulated. The Welfare State had removed much of the sense of insecurity and discontent that had fueled the Communist movement. In urban areas, the traditional working class subculture with its own clubs and newspapers had been submerged by the middle class values of suburban living. Like the rest of Western Europe, Finland had become an affluent consumer society in which concepts like the class struggle and the dictatorship of the proletariat have lost their relevance for all except a handful of believers.

With the collapse of the Polish economy and stagnation in the Soviet Union the promise of a better future lost its credibility. In the 1980s, the Communist parties in Western Europe faced the thankless task of trying to persuade voters that the Socialism they were offering was something different from the system existing in Eastern Europe. Throughout Western Europe the Communist movement, plagued by internal divisions, was losing votes. Even more important, it ceased to be a significant intellectual force and no longer attracted young people.

The change in the climate of opinion in Europe as a whole has been profound. In the West, the contest between the two systems no longer preoccupies politicians and commentators. Now the Soviet Union is on the defensive. The new generation of leaders under Mikhail Gorbachev has inherited a stagnant economy unable for long to sustain the gigantic military machine of a global superpower. The Soviet Union must try to catch up with the West in technological development. But Western Europe is facing the other way. The demand for greater unity is heard again, but no longer to defend democracy against Communism, but to meet the economic challenge from the United States and Japan.

In Finland, the number of seats held by the Communists and their allies in Parliament fell from 40 out of 200 in 1975 to 27 in 1983. The Conservative party increased its strength from 36 to 44 in the same period. In the elections of March 1987, for the first time two rival Communist parties put forward candidates. The result was a further decline of Communist strength. The »eurocommunist» party was reduced to 16 seats and the »dogmatists» to four. The victors were the conservatives who increased their share to 53 seats — only two less than the Social-Democrats. In May 1987 the Conservative politician Harri Holkeri formed a coalition government of his own party and the Social-Democrats.

The sharp edges of social conflict have been blunted. As differences in income, education, housing and life styles have been reduced, the political parties have difficulties in finding issues on which they could disagree. The Conservatives have years ago suppressed any impulse to demand a dismantling of the Welfare State. The Social- Democratic party made its U-turn in economic thinking well ahead of the Socialist parties in France or Sweden and has trimmed its program to fit the realities of a market economy. As both Right and Left compete for votes among the same groups of uncommitted voters, their slogans sometimes seem interchangeable.

In these conditions consensus has become the watchword of Finnish politics. Economic and social policy is shaped in negotiations between the leading political parties and the organizations representing the interests of wage-earners and employers as well as farmers. Decisionmaking by consensus served the country well in the late 1970s and early 1980s. The economy was managed with reasonable success: growth rates were high and unemployment well below the average in Western Europe. But there are obvious drawbacks. Power is shifted away from Parliament, and responsibility is widely spread. Left-wing critics claim that the more radical ideas are eliminated without real public debate, while the complaint from the Right is that incomes policy is too rigid in a time of rapid technological change. The voters, especially the younger age groups, become frustrated by the lack of a clear-cut choice in elections. The endless process of haggling and compromise leading to consensus takes the drama out of politics: only bread, no circus.

Yet there can be no doubt that Finnish politics will continue to be a search for consensus. This is, after all, built into the Finnish system of government. But

6 Finland: Myth and Reality

it also reflects the realities of our time. The power of organized economic interests is a fact which cannot be ignored: parliamentarism and corporatism must come to terms with each other. At the same time the internationalization of economic activity continues at an ever faster pace. A small, open market economy like that of Finland's must adjust to the trends prevailing in the world economy. The margin of independent action left to Finnish decisionmakers is narrow indeed. It makes sense to try to reach a wide consensus on how to use that margin, rather than leave the decision to a confrontation between opposing interests and chance majorities. It is a boring way to run a country, but then the political process is meant to produce rationality and stability, not entertainment.

X
Democracy and Development

Democracy, it is often said, is a luxury only the wealthy nations can afford. The leaders of backward and poor peoples must be excused for using dictatorial methods of government; there is no other way to economic development.

This view, often expressed by persons who in their own countries are staunch defenders of democracy, is contradicted by the Finnish experience. The Finnish people have transformed a desperately poor, backward and isolated agrarian society into a modern state with an advanced economy which today ranks ninth among the wealthiest nations of the world, and they have done so by their own efforts, without any foreign economic assistance, while maintaining a democratic system of government. Yet it would be misleading to claim that the success of Finland has been entirely due to reliance on free enterprise and market forces. It is rather the result of a combination of private effort and public action, individual initiative and cooperative endeavour, which does not easily fit into any of the categories normally used to describe different economic systems.

In the 19th century, the Finnish people, in the words of the national poet J. L. Runeberg, had to »Wrest their bread from ice and snow». In the poorest areas bread was often made from flour mixed with pine bark. In the famine years of 1867-68 some hundred thousand people, eight per cent of the total population, died of starvation or disease.

Industrialization developed in Finland later than in the other Scandinavian countries or Western Europe in general. In 1880, more than 90 per cent of the total population of two million still lived in rural areas. In economic terms, Finland in the 19th century was like the backward agrarian societies of Eastern Europe. But there were important differences. In cultural and social terms, Finland was a Scandinavian country. The Lutheran church had educated the people in the spirit of the »Protestant work ethic». A system of public education was established as early as in 1866, and a high a rate of literacy was achieved in the 19th century. Since the nobility was small in numbers and possessed no great wealth, education was the main means of social advancement.

A crucial factor in the country's economic development was the ownership of land. In Finland, in contrast to Eastern Europe, there have never been vast estates owned by powerful nobles employing large numbers of tenants or serfs. The greater part of the land has always been owned by independent farmers. As a result ownership of the country's national wealth − the forests − is widely distributed. Most of the forests, the »green gold» of Finland, still is owned by the farmers. This is a fact of cardinal importance for an understanding of how Finland developed in the 20th century. It meant that, as industries using wood as raw material began to develop in the 1890s in response to growing demand in Britain and elsewhere in Europe, the Finnish farmers were brought into the sphere of a capitalist market economy depending on export trade.

Industrialization did not develop fast enough to absorb the whole surplus population of the rural areas, nor did emigration to America solve the problem. (In 1850 − 1910 Finnish emigration reached a total of 7,7 per cent of the population in 1910, while in Sweden the corresponding figure was 17,5.) The rural proletariat of tenant farmers and landless labourers was one of the driving forces behind the revolutionary movement in 1918, while the more prosperous farmers formed the backbone of the White army.

After the civil war, the victorious side had the foresight to carry out a far-reaching land reform which, in 1918 and 1922, created close to 100 000 new farms. The reform went against the grain of economic trends in Western Europe where the farming population was rapidly declining. Many of the new farms were too small to be profitable and could not have managed at all without the services of the cooperative movement. But the benefits in terms of social and political stability were of incalculable value. Without farm reform the Finnish people could hardly have achieved national unity in the short time that was available before the great storm.

At the end of the Second World War Finland once again carried out a major New Deal by resettling the population of the lost province of Karelia − 436 000 people or twelve per cent of the nation. Virtually no one had stayed behind the new frontier; the Russians had taken over a land emptied of human life, a province of ghosts. In the aftermath of the Second World War, when millions had fled or had been forcibly evicted from their homes, the fate of the Finnish Karelians received little notice outside the country. Yet there has been no parallel elsewhere to the voluntary and spontaneous exodus of the entire population of the province, induced neither by persuasion by the Finnish side nor by force or terror on the part of the Russians. The manner in which the Karelians were received was also unique. They were not herded into camps but were billeted, family by family, on the rest of the population throughout the country. And they were compensated for their loss of property, not only in money but also in land for those who were farmers. The resettlement and absorption of the Karelians placed on the Finnish economy an immense burden which is almost impossible to calculate in money. An Act of Parliament passed in 1945 created some 142 000 new holdings out of 2,8 million hectars of land, mostly by compulsory purchase. Finland was the only OECD country where the farm population increased after the Second World War. Again, economic considerations were set aside in the interest of maintaining national unity and social cohesion.

Life in Finland thus was determined by a set of priorities which in important respects differed from those prevailing in Western Europe. As a result, the economy of Finland in 1950 still had some of the characteristics of what today would be called a developing country. Close to half of the total population — 47 per cent — was still supported by farming and forestry, while the corresponding figure in Sweden was 20, in Denmark 24 and Norway 26. The forest industry accounted for four fifths of all exports: Finland was a one-crop country at the mercy of every shift in the international market for timber or pulp and paper. The domestic market was too small to stimulate an industrial expansion, while access to external markets was still restricted by the many trade barriers that divided postwar Europe.

The first opening was provided, surprisingly, by the war reparations demanded by the Soviet Union. At the Teheran Conference in 1943, Winston Churchill had tried to dissuade Stalin from asking heavy reparations from Finland, conceding, however, that »the Finns might cut down a few trees». But Stalin was not intrested in trees, of which Russia herself had more than enough. He insisted that two- thirds of the goods to be delivered as reparations by Finland were to be ships, machinery and other engineering products which Finland had never produced in sufficient quantities even for her own use, and only one third in timber and paper products. To meet this demand Finland had to double the capacity of her shipbuilding and engineering industries at an enforced pace: a task that was the economic equivalent of the war itself. A combination of public and private enterprise was used to build up the industrial capacity required. The reparations amounted to roughly ten per cent of the gross national income in 1945, a proportion four times as much as that of the German gross national income devoted to reparations in 1925-30.

Payment of the war indemnity brought about a change in the structure of industry and, as a consequence, in the pattern of the foreign trade of Finland. Once the indemnity had been paid off in 1952, the Soviet Union began to buy from Finland the goods it had received free of charge until then. To suspicious minds it looked like a devilish plot designed to absorb Finland by economic means. Once again, Western obeservers underestimated the vitality of the market system. In fact the Soviet share of Finland's foreign trade has remained remarkably stable at an an average of twenty per cent or slightly less over a period of more than thirty years.

Credits received from the United States helped Finland to pay the reparations on time. While American diplomats in their reports expressed doubt about Finland's chances of survival as an independent state, the country's credit rating remained high. Her reputation had been established in the early 1930s, when the Finnish government had decided to pay back the loan received from the United States immeadiately after the First World War. Had two or three other European states taken similar action, the Finnish decision would hardly have been noticed. But as it happens, Finland was the only one to pay back the American credits, and this turned what had been considered a routine matter into one of the most successful public relations operations of all time. Soon every schoolboy in America knew at least one thing about Finland — that it was the only country that paid its debts. Repayments were streched out to last as long as possible. Even at the worst time of the Second World War, when Finnish-American relations were at their lowest point, the Finnish ambassador made his annual call at the United States Treasury Department waving a cheque for the benefit of press photographers. Finally, at the end of the 1940s, the loan was converted into a fund for the financing of scholarships for Finns studying in the United States.

Having declined to take part in the Marshall Plan, Finland tried to turn her self-denial to some political advantage. Making a virtue of necessity, Finland proclaimed a policy of not seeking aid from any quarter, thus adding a new dimension to her image as the only country that had paid back its war debts. When President Kekkonen visited the United States in October 1961 an American newspaper described him as the only foreign statesman who had come to the UnitedStates without stretching out his hand — palm upward. And Secretary of State Dean Rusk said after his talk with the Finnish President that he was unaccustomed to visitors who did not ask for anything.

As a consequence, however, Finland was left behind Western Europe in economic development. Apart from missing out on American aid, Finland was excluded from the Organization for European Economic Cooperation (OEEC), the forerunner of today's OECD.(Finland joined the OECD in 1967.) Finnish policy had to employ a great deal of ingenuity to find round-about

ways of sharing in the continuing process of liberaliz-
ation of trade. For instance, when the OEEC countries
had formed the European Payments Union in order to
free currency transactions between them, Finland
founded in 1957 her own payments union, »The
Helsinki Club», to which all OEEC countries adhered.

Scandinavian cooperation at one time was thought to
provide a possible backdoor to West European integration, or a substitute for it. As early as in 1954 the
four Nordic countries, Denmark, Finland, Norway and
Sweden, agreed to the free movement of labour between them. Ever since citizens of the four countries
have been able to seek employment in anyone of them
without the restrictions normally applied to foreigners.
In 1956, Finland also joined the Nordic Council, a joint
organ of the Parliaments of the five Nordic countries
(the four mentioned above plus Iceland), which had
initiated negotiations for the creation of a Scandinavian customs union. In 1959 the plan for a customs
union was virtually completed. But it was too late. The
plan was still-born. It had been superceded by the
larger plan of a European Free Trade Association –
EFTA – comprising Denmark, Norway and Sweden
as well as Great Britain, Austria, Switzerland and
Portugal. Its goal was to abolish within ten years customs duties on industrial goods and remove other barriers restricting trade between its member states. It
was Britain's answer to General de Gaulle's refusal to
accept her into the European Economic Community.

Since Britain at the time was Finland's biggest cus-
tomer and the other countries of EFTA included some
of Finland's main competitors in the British market, it
was clear from the outset that Finland had to join the
group. But the pattern of Finland's foreign trade differed in one important respect from that of the other
Nordic countries: this was the extent of her trade with

the Soviet Union. Moscow considered both the European Economic Community and EFTA hostile organizations that discriminated against Soviet exports, while EFTA insisted on terms of membership which would have made it difficult for Finland to maintain her share of the Soviet market. After a complex negotiation the Finnish government succeeded in reconciling the interests of its two trading partners and joined the Free Trade Area in the beginning of 1961.

During the latter part of 1960s a new effort was made to create a Nordic economic bloc, »Nordek», but once again the rug was pulled out from under its feet when Britain joined the European Economic Community, drawing Denmark with her. Finland and Sweden decided that membership in the EEC was incompatible with their policy of neutrality, while in Norway membership was rejected by a referendum. All three states, along with Austria and Switzerland, concluded free trade agreements with the EEC.

The Nordic countries have in fact achieved a high degree of economic unity, but as a by-product of the wider movement toward integration in Western Europe as a whole, rather than as a result of separate Nordic action. In cultural and social terms, however, indeed in all that touches the life of the individual citizen, the integration of the Nordic countries has been carried further than between any other group of independent states.

Membership in the EFTA and free trade with the EEC put an end to the relative isolation of Finland. As part of the West-European economic system the country was rapidly transformed. It caught up with Western Europe in one great leap. The industrial development that in other countries had taken several decades was accomplished in ten to fifteen years.

Finland today is an industrial consumer society with

an expanding service sector and highly developed welfare services. According to World Bank statistics, Finland's gross domestic product per capita in 1984 was US 10 740, which was less than the figure for Switzerland, the Unites States, Norway, Sweden, Canada, Denmark, Australia and West Germany, but more than France, Netherlands, Austria, Britain, Belgium and Italy. The country has been discovered by the international investors who believe they can find bargains on the Helsinki Stock Exchange.

Finland does, however, retain certain features which distinguish her from the other Nordic countries. One is the continued importance of farming. True, the farm population has fallen from 32 per cent in 1960 to around 9 per cent in the 1980s. But the proportion is still somewhat higher than in the other Nordic countries. Finns on the whole agree that it would not be in the national interest to let market forces reduce farming much further. A high degree of selfsufficiency in food production is considered necessary. But there are also other, less tangible but in some ways even more important considerations. Forestry would suffer, the very character of the country would change, even national security could ultimately be impaired, if large parts of Finland were depopulated.

Another characteristic feature of Finland is the continued importance of the forest industry in economic life. The industrial structure has become more diversified and the country no longer is as dependent on the forest industry as it used to be. The forest industry's share of exports has dropped from 70 per cent in 1960 to around 40 per cent in the 1980s and now is equal to that of the metal and engineering industry. But as a net earner of foreign currency the forest industry continues to lead the field. Significantly, its own structure is changing, as investments in recent years have been directed almost entirely to more highly processed types of printing and writing paper, in respect of which Finland has reached a 25 per cent share of world trade.

Another difference between Finland and the other Nordic countries is in the balance between the public and the private sector. On the whole Finnish society is more conservative. The Social-Democratic party has not been as dominant as in the other Nordic countries, and as a result the Finnish Welfare State has a somewhat different shape. The level of public spending as a proportion of GDP in Finland is just above 40 per cent, which is about the OECD average — that is, clearly lower than in the other Nordic countries. Consequently the level of taxation is also lower. As a result of the consensus reached in the latter half of the 1970s between the Social-Democrats and the Center parties, the growth of public spending was slowed down and the gross tax ratio actually reduced. Thus Finland escaped from being sucked into the vicious circle of growing budget deficits and rising public debt that afflicted most West European countries at that time. But in the 1980s public spending has again been rising somewhat.

The movement of labour between Finland and Sweden illustrates the relative success of Finnish economic policy. In 1966-70, 125 000 Finns moved to Sweden to work, while only 42 000 returned to Finland. At the time industrial wages were considerably higher in Sweden. In the period 1976-80, 66 000 moved to Sweden and 31 000 returned. In 1980 industrial wages in Finland caught up with the Swedish level and moved ahead in 1980-85, and in that period more people returned from Sweden to Finland than moved in the other direction.

Finally, the structure of her foreign trade, as has been pointed out, makes Finland different from the other Nordic countries. About two-thirds of her exports go to Western Europe, but the Soviet market is also important. Exports to the Soviet Union were twelve per cent of total exports in 1970, but then received a strong boost from the rise in the price of oil. This is due to the nature of the trade between Finland and the Soviet Union. It is based on bilateral clearing agreements − a form of barter. This means that Finland can sell only as much as she buys from the Soviet Union, and her imports consist mostly of oil and other raw materials. In the late 1970s and the first half of the 1980s, Finland was able to pay for the greater part of her oil imports through the exports of industrial products, mainly ships and machinery. At the height of the oil boom the Soviet share of Finnish exports went up to 26 per cent. As oil prices began to fall in the mid-eighties, Finnish exports to the Soviet Union declined accordingly. Efforts to diversify imports from the Soviet Union have had little success, and the inability of the Soviet Union to offer industrial goods attractive to Finnish byers sets a ceiling on Finnish-Soviet trade that is not likely to be lifted in the foreseeable future.

The possible political consequences of the trade with the Soviet Union caused a great deal of uneasiness in Finland in the immediate post-war period. In 1949-50, and again in 1958, delays in trade talks with Moscow were perceived as political pressure, though they were never explicitly linked to any political demands by the Soviet government. President Paasikivi said in 1950 that exports to the Soviet Union should not exceed twenty per cent of total exports, and this happens to be roughly the annual average of the last three decades, although the limit has been set by economic realities rather than by political design. But much has changed since Paasikivi's days, on both sides. Finnish-Soviet trade does have political aspects, but they are more complex than is commonly believed.

The issue must be seen in the wider context of the development of world economic relations. In theory, Marxism- Leninism regards trade primarily as a tool of policy, while the Western view is that business is business and should not be mixed with politics. In actual fact, however, it is the Soviet Union which today clamours for an end to political obstacles to trade, while in the West trade with the Soviet bloc is discussed in political terms: either as a means to enmesh the Soviet Union in a network of mutual dependence or as an instrument of pressure designed to change Soviet political behaviour. This reversal of roles is not so paradoxical as it may seem. It reflects the balance of economic power between the two systems. East-West trade is much more important to the Soviet Union than it is for the West. Indeed, Gorbachev's economic reform requires a greater Soviet involvement in world trade, including in the longer run participation in the principal international economic oganizations like the International Monetary Fund and the World Bank as well as GATT.

Seen against this background trade with Finland must have a special value for Soviet policymakers. Since it is based on long-term agreements, imports of high quality Finnish products, like for instance ice-breakers and other ships designed for Arctic conditions as well as turn-key industrial projects, have become an integral part of Soviet economic planning. Unlike trade with NATO countries, trade with Finland is not subject to ups and downs in political relations. It is, from the Soviet view, a show-case of the benefits of economic cooperation between the Soviet Union and a capitalist country. Both sides have acquired a strong interest in maintaining the present trade relationship. Disrupting it by the use of trade as a means of political pressure could bring the Soviet Union no conceivable political gain of such importance that it would outweigh the damage caused to Soviet efforts to present itself to the Western world as a reliable trading partner.

Under the leadership of Mikhail Gorbachev the Soviet Union now offers Western businesses the opportunity to start »joint ventures» with Soviet enterprises. The first such joint venture between a Finnish firm and its Soviet partner was started in 1987. But the gulf between two different economic systems cannot easily be bridged. Unless the Soviet system is changed much more radically than today seems likely, integration between the two systems in the Western sense must be excluded.

The real challenge to Finland in the next decades can be deduced from the following figures: The Finnish population is 0,1 percent of the world total, but the Gross Domestic Product of Finland is 0,5 per cent and her exports 0,7 per cent of the world total. In order to maintain her people in the style they are accustomed to, Finland must keep pace with the dynamic technological change within the Western world. The slogan »Export or die» is already out of date; it is now »Internationalize or die». For enterprises in small countries with a small domestic market and limited human and material resources, this means increasing participation in international operations of all kinds, finding niches in the world market for their own products or services, developing a high degree of know-how in selective fields – in a word, specialization.

Every step in this direction makes the Finnish economy more dependent on the international environment. Thus progress within the European Economic Communities toward the goal of creating a unified market by 1992 presents Finland with a complex set of problems. In this respect the four neutral member of the European Free Trade Area (Austria, Finland, Sweden and Switzerland) are all in the same boat. Since membership in the EEC would be incompatible with neutrality, they must find other ways to make sure that changes within the Common Market do not raise new obstacles to free trade with the EFTA. (The fifth member of the EFTA, Norway, as a NATO country is not of course inhibited by political considerations from joining the EEC; indeed it is possible that political motives might induce her to seek membership in the Community.) In the field of technological research, forms of cooperation covering both the EEC and the EFTA – the Eureka program for instance – have already been established. What lies ahead is a continuous process of adjustment, probably extending far beyond the target year of 1992 and involving literally hundreds of practical measures affecting the way industry and business operate.

In Finland, joining this process has not required any dramatic policy decision. Rather, it follows as a matter of course from the fact that since the late 1950s Finland has been an integral part of the »European Economic Space», a term designed to encompass both the EEC and the EFTA which, while different in structure, have a common interest in preserving freedom of trade throughout Western Europe. To keep up with developments within this Space is to maintain continuity of Finnish policy; to fall behind would have consequences wholly unacceptable to the great majority of Finns.

XI
Code Word Neutrality

Neutrality as a concept of policy is usually defined in negative terms, as a refusal to join alliances or to take sides: hardly a slogan to make your blood boil. Yet in Finland at times the very word has stirred up deep emotions, as for instance when President Urho Kekkonen declared that Finnish neutrality was the essence of his life's work, which he would defend to his last breath.

To an outsider, such a passionate commitment to what commonly is considered a posture of cool detachment may seem strange. But to the Finnish people at the time it did not sound strange at all. Kekkonen made his statement in November 1961 in the shadow of the Berlin crisis. It was a moment of extreme tension in Europe: President Kennedy had put the odds of a nuclear war at one to five. Moscow had just invited the Finnish government to enter into military consultations under the 1948 Treaty to consider joint measures against the threat posed by aggressive West German policies. It was widely feared, in Finland and elsewhere, that such consultations would compromise Finland's neutrality or even undermine her independence. In this situation Kekkonen's pledge carried a message that went beyond a simple statement of neutrality: it was his way of saying no.

Neutrality always implies the rejection of another alternative. In theory, a small state lying between two rival military blocs can choose between joining either bloc or staying neutral. In practice, however, it is inconceivable that a state could choose either of two alliances. For reasons of geopolitics or ideology, normally only one can be an acceptable alternative. Thus a state which chooses neutrality rejects the alternative of joining one of the alliances. But the alternative usually remains available as a fall-back position for use in the event that neutrality cannot be maintained.

The position of Sweden during the Cold War is a case in point. The alternatives for Sweden at the end of the 1940s were neutrality or membership in NATO. By staying neutral Sweden said no to NATO. It followed that the Western Powers regarded Swedish neutrality with displeasure, while the Soviet Union praised it. But when Hungary in 1956 declared its neutrality, the West applauded the decision, but the Soviet Union suppressed it by force. In both cases the potential alternative to neutrality determined the attitudes of the Big Powers. Since Sweden was considered a potential ally of the West, her neutrality was counted as a defeat for NATO and a victory for the Soviet Union, while Hungarian neutrality would have been considered a loss for the Soviet Union and a gain for the West.

It is an old story: As Macchiavelli put it, »The one who is not your friend will want you to remain neutral, and the one who is your friend will require you to declare yourself by taking arms.»

In the case of Sweden the NATO option remained open, at least in theory. During the Cold War period, when Swedish neutrality was often criticized in the West on moral grounds, Swedes used to defend themselves with reference to Finland: Swedish neutrality, they claimed, helped Finland maintain her independence. The implication was that a change in the situation of Finland might cause a revision of Swedish policy. The unspoken assumption of Swedish policy was that the country could come under threat only from the East and, if attacked, would seek support from the West.

Austria's road to neutrality was quite different, but the end result in essence similar to the Swedish position. By adopting permanent neutrality Austria persuaded the Soviet Union to agree to end the occupation. From the Soviet point of view, Austrian neutrality is in effect a commitment on the part of the Austrians not to join the Western Alliance. It follows that Moscow has always insisted on a strict interpretation of Austrian neutrality, while the West has shown little interest in this matter, knowing that any departure from neutrality could only be in favour of the West.

The position of Finland is fundamentally different from that of the other neutral states in Europe. In a formal sense, the difference is that Finland has a security treaty with the Soviet Union, while the other neutral states have no such treaty commitments. But the Finnish-Soviet Treaty only spells out what is implicit in the relationship between the other neutral states and the Western Alliance. The real difference is that, like Austria, Sweden and Switzerland, Finland is a Western country ideologically and culturally, and part of the Western economic system, but in the geopolitical structure of Europe she is placed in an area which has a vital importance for the security of the Soviet Union. The Finnish policy of neutrality is designed to resolve the latent conflict between ideological ties and strategic realities inherent in the country's situation. Unlike the other neutral states, Finland cannot lean on historical or cultural affinities or shared values. She must base her security on an unsentimental calculation of the national interest.

The limits of ideological solidarity were revealed to the Finnish people in 1939. Chamberlain put it bluntly in his famous speech about Czechoslovakia – »the far-away country of which we know nothing»:

»However much we may sympathize with a small nation confronted by a big and powerful neighbour, we cannot in all circumstances undertake to involve the whole British empire in war simply on her account.»

There had been, in the 1920s and 1930s, vague discussions about a Nordic defence union, but defence against whom? The Finns feared Russia, the Danes Germany; the Swedes could not make up their minds which to fear more; the Norwegians believed they need not fear either. The more specific plan of a joint Finnish-Swedish defence of the Åland Islands foundered on the unwillingness of Sweden to risk a conflict with the Soviet Union. The Anglo-French plan to save Finland in 1940 turned out to be a ruse. After the Winter War even Marshal Mannerheim, a man singularly free of sentimentality, was moved to declare that »Finland had paid her debt to the West to the last drop».

During the Second Round of the Finnish-Soviet war, the Western Allies in their treatment of Finland showed a cynical disregard for the democratic values they were supposed to be fighting for. As the Second World War ended, there could be no illusions in Finland about relying on the support of the Western democracies against Soviet power. As early as in 1943 Urho Kekkonen, in a speech in Stockholm, pointed out that as an outpost of a Western alliance Finland would always be the first to be overrun or sacrificed in a conflict, yet too weak to influence decisions on war and peace. He concluded that Finland had to adopt a policy of neutrality, but one that unlike the pre-war policy could gain the confidence of the Soviet Union.

For ten years after the end of the war neutrality remained an unspoken aspiration of Finnish policy. There was no place for neutral countries in Stalin's world-view: those who were not for the Soviet Union were against it. In the West, John Foster Dulles called neutrality an immoral position for a free nation to take. To the small nations of Europe neutrality seemed an illusion. In the light of the experiences of the 1930s it was believed that only collective defence under the protection of the United States could deter the Soviet Union or, failing that, ensure that effective military assistance could be obtained without fatal delay. Otherwise, it was feared, the smaller democracies would be forced, one by one, to submit to Soviet domination. In any case, Finland seemed doomed to remain firmly chained to the Soviet security system, with the Soviet forces at their Porkkala base standing guard over her.

Yet even in those years, as Europe was being ever more firmly divided into two opposing camps, Finland managed to practice a policy of neutrality without actually saying so. Having said no to the invitation from George Marshall on the ground that his plan had become a matter of dispute between the Big Powers, President Paasikivi in November in 1954 was confronted with an invitation from Vyacheslav Molotov to a European security conference. Its purpose, according to the Soviet proposal, was to create a European security system within which Germany could be unified. The invitation had been sent to all European states as well as to the United States and Canada, but it became immediately clear that the West would reject the Soviet proposal.

The world watched with interest which side Finland would take. The Finnish reply was positive: Yes, Finland was in favour of a European security system and would be happy to join a conference of the states invited by Moscow. What was not said but implied was that Finland would join only if all those invited would accept. Since this condition was not fulfilled, Finland did not send a delegation to the Moscow Conference which, as it turned out, was the first formal step toward the creation of the Warsaw Pact. As in the old joke about the difference between a lady and a diplomat, Finland had found a way of saying yes and meaning no.

Another crucial test for Finland was the German issue. There was no ready-made formula for dealing with it on the basis of neutrality. The West claimed the government of the Federal Republic of Germany was the sole legitimate representative of the German people as a whole, while the Soviet Union insisted there existed two separate sovereign German states. To recognize the Federal Republic was to accept the Western claim; to recognize two German states was to side with the Soviet Union and risk economic retaliation from the West. The dilemma was solved by Finland in a manner that probably has no precedent in the history of international relations. Finland recognized neither the Federal Republic nor the Democratic Republic. Instead of diplomatic relations she maintained trade missions in both and through these conducted business equally with East and West. Neither side was happy with this arrangement, but both accepted it. For the West, the important thing was that Finland refused to recognize the East German state; the East Germans on their part made the most of the fact that Finland accorded both German states equal treatment. Any attempt to fit the Finnish policy into the framework of international law would be a desperate undertaking. But in practice it served Finland well and was continued until 1972, when the existence of two German states was recognized by the West.

By such evasive manouvers the Finnish government succeeded in staying uncommitted in a divided Europe. But Finland was not yet recognized as a neutral country, nor did President Paasikivi use that word to define Finland's position. The Soviet base at Porkkala »cast its shadow over Finnish independence». In the West, the Finnish-Soviet Treaty of 1948 was not accepted at face value, and in Finland, too, suspicions with regard to Soviet intentions ran deep.

At Paasikivi's insistence, the duration of the Treaty had been limited to ten years. This meant it was to expire two years after the end of Paasikivi's term of office, and as the moment of his retirement drew closer, the aged President used to meditate, as his diary reveals, about what his successor might do about the Treaty: Should it be extended as it was or should an attempt be made to amend it?

Obviously, the Soviet leaders, too, had been speculating about what would happen to the Treaty in 1958, and they were well aware that no one could be sure of who might be elected to succeed Paasikivi. So they decided to act while Paasikivi was still in power in order to ensure the continuity of the policy set by him. In the late summer of 1955, six months before the presidential election was due, Paasikivi received Moscow's offer: The Soviet government was prepared immediately to return to Finland the Porkkala base, if Finland in turn agreed to extend the validity of the Treaty of 1948 for another twenty years. Paasikivi did not hesitate to accept. In September 1955 he went to Moscow himself to attend the signing of the agreement to cancel the lease and to extend the Treaty. This, his seventh trip to the Soviet capital in the course of sixteen years, was the first one, as he himself put it, from which he returned satisfied.

Of course the return of Porkkala had wider implications. In the beginning of 1955 Nikita Khrushchev had become the dominant figure in the Soviet leadership, and he was giving Soviet foreign policy a new look. He abandoned Stalin's thesis of a world rigidly divided into two hostile camps. In his view, those who were not for the Soviet Union need not necessarily be against it. He made his peace with Tito and courted Nehru. He agreed to withdraw the Soviet occupation forces from Austria in return for an Austrian pledge of neutrality. He returned to China the Soviet bases in Dairen and Port Arthur, and urged the United States to give up its bases in foreign countries.

In the West, the return of Porkkala was generally dismissed as a cheap gesture. Obviously the base had lost its usefulness. It had never actually served a strategic purpose. In October 1939 Stalin had argued the Soviet Union needed forward bases on both shores of the Gulf of Finland so that entry to the Gulf could be denied to hostile warships by coastal artillery fire, as had been possible in Czarist times. At the time Finnish military experts had tried to convince him that his strategic thinking was out of date, and the experiences of the Second World War had proved them right: once the Germans had taken the Southern shore of the Gulf, the Soviet base in Finland, acquired at the cost of the Winter War, had to be abandoned. In the nuclear age Porkkala was of course quite irrelevant to the defence of Leningrad. By giving it up the Soviet Union had given up nothing in terms of the global balance of power.

For Finland, however, the departure of the Soviet forces from Porkkala in January 1956 was an event of profound significance. Had the Soviet Union had aggressive designs on Finland, Porkkala could easily have been used for pressure or blackmail. So long as the Russians stayed in Porkkala, Finland was like a prisoner free on probation. By abandoning the base Chruchev showed the Soviet Union had come to trust Finland to keep her end of the bargain struck in 1948 and no longer felt the need of keeping its watch at Porkkala. The concession lent powerful support to Paasikivi's thesis that Soviet policy with regard to Finland was defensive and that the line he had taken was the best way of securing Finnish independence.

Why then did the Soviet Union still keep the province of Karelia? Stalin had argued that the Finnish border north of Leningrad had to be moved further away because the city was »within the range of modern artillery». This made no sense in the age of ballistic missiles. Many Karelians were still dreaming of a return, and the matter was raised by the Finnish government leaders in the Moscow talks in September 1955. But the answer was a blank no. True, the Soviet Union no longer needed Karelia for its defence. But a revision of the frontiers established as a result of the Second World War could be a dangerous precedent. The Poles, the Rumanians, the Japanese, above all the Chinese would be encouraged to press their claims.

The territorial issue was not raised again. In the course of time Karelia has become sublimated in the minds of the Finnish people into a cultural concept. Today Finland would be acutely embarrassed by a Soviet offer to return the province. Who would go to live there and how would a resettlement be financed? Possession of territory has ceased to be the valued prize for which nations have spilt so much blood.

The elimination of the Soviet base not only stabilized Finnish-Soviet relations but also transformed Finland's international position. There was an obvious parallel between Soviet actions in Austria and in Finland in 1955. So long as the Finnish government could not claim full control over its territory it had not been in the position of asking other states to respect its neutrality in the event of war. The removal of the Soviet base opened the way to international recognition of Finnish neutrality. It was logical, therefore, that the XXth Congress of the Soviet Communist Party in February 1956, a month after the evacuation of Porkkala, was the first occasion on which Finland was called a neutral state in an official Soviet statement.

By encouraging neutrality and nonalignment Khrushchev was hoping to ease the confrontation between East and West. How far was he prepared to go? There was much speculation on this point at the time. Even John Foster Dulles saw merit in neutrality, so long as it spread on the other side of the dividing line in Europe. In American comments Finland was made to appear like a poor man's Statue of Liberty transmitting muted signals of hope to »the captive nations» of Eastern Europe. If Finland could be neutral without posing a risk to Soviet security, why not Hungary or Czechoslovakia or Poland?

Obviously the question was asked in Moscow, too. Khrushchev later revealed in his conversations with Finnish representatives that the withdrawal of Soviet troops from Porkkala and from Austria had been opposed by Molotov who probably represented the views of the security policy establishment in the Soviet Union. Khrushchev's critics must have felt a grim satisfaction when news of the Hungarian declaration of neutrality reached Moscow. In October 1956 Khrushchev's vision of a neutral zone separating NATO and Warsaw Pact forces in Central Europe turned into the nightmare of Soviet tanks crushing the Hungarian freedom fighters. But by that time Porkkala was in Finnish hands.

XII
The Paasikivi-Kekkonen Line

Having led his people to the promised land of neutrality Paasikivi retired from the presidency in March 1956 and died before the end of the year at the age of 86. His successor Urho Kekkonen pledged himself to continue Paasikivi's policy. The phrase »Paasikivi-Kekkonen line» was coined to reassure the Soviet leaders. Yet the two men were very different in practically every respect. Paasikivi had taken public office for granted. He had never been a candidate in a parliamentary election, and in the presidential election of 1950 his victory had been a foregone conclusion. Kekkonen was born, literally, in a log cabin in north-eastern Finland. He worked his way through university and fought his first election campaign as a candidate of the Agrarian party in 1937. Till the end of his days he regarded himself as a champion of the poor against the privileged. But he was a nationalist not a socialist. Social justice and equality were necessary to make the Finnish nation strong enough to survive as an independent state. The function of the state was to protect those who were left behind by market forces and to resolve potential conflicts between different groups in the interest of national unity.

Before the Second World War Kekkonen had shared the militant anti-Russian attitudes of his generation, and at the end of the Winter War in March 1940 he had been one of the few politicians who had opposed the Peace Treaty with the Soviet Union. But disillusionment with Western policies brought him to the conviction that Finland had to find a way to come to terms with Soviet power. After the war he emerged as a leading exponent of the Paasikivi Line, and in 1956 he campaigned for the presidency as the man best fitted to take over Paasikivi's role as guarantor of good relations with the Soviet Union.

There could be no doubt that Kekkonen enjoyed the confidence of Moscow. In their dealings with other countries the Soviet leaders tend to place their trust in personal relationships rather than institutional arrangements: an inclination hardly in keeping with Marxist-Leninist doctrine but rather a relic of the Russian tradition of autocracy. Such personal relationships are not based on ideological affinities but on the realities of power. Moscow wants to deal with the man who can deliver his end of the bargain. In Finland as in France, after the end of the Second World War Soviet policy relied on men of the Right: first Mannerheim, then Paasikivi. Kekkonen, too, had pledged himself to defend what was called the bourgeois structure of Finnish society.

In a democracy, such a personalization of foreign relations has its obvious drawbacks. Continuity in foreign policy becomes dependent on the vagaries of the electoral process; criticism of the person in charge may seem an attack on the substance of policy and normal rivalry between politicl parties a challenge to national unity. During the first term of Kekkonen's presidency Finland was indeed convulsed by an internal struggle for power. Kekkonen did not start off with the personal authority his predecessor had had. He was the kind of political leader who inspires absolute loyalty and devotion on the part of his followers, but also arouses bitter hostility among opponents. In the eyes of his supporters he was the saviour of Finnish independence, not just the best man but the only man who could convince Moscow to leave Finland alone; his critics called him an opportunist who had made a deal with the Soviets in order to maintain his personal power. The opposition claimed that it, too, supported the Paasikivi Line, but could not trust Kekkonen to conduct foreign policy in the national interest. But Khrushchev, in 1960, declared that »whoever is for Kekkonen is for friendship with the Soviet Union and whoever is against Kekkonen is against friendship with the Soviet Union».

In the autumn of 1958, at a moment of East-West tension over Berlin, Moscow froze its relations with Finland in a demonstration of displeasure with political developments there. Three years later, during another Berlin crisis, the Soviet call for military talks under the 1948 Treaty struck Finland in the midst of an electoral contest in which Kekkonen was challenged by a broad coalition including both the Conservatives and the major part of the Social- Democratic party: strange bedfellows united solely by the desire to unseat Kekkonen. But the President travelled to the Soviet Union and persuaded Khruschev not to insist on military talks − a triumph that ensured him a clear majority in the presidential elections in January 1962.

The charge of interference in Finland's domestic affairs was dismissed by Khrushchev with the bland remark that of course the Finnish people were free to elect anyone they wished, but the Soviet government was entitled to draw its conclusions and determine its policy with regard to Finland accordingly. He could have quoted John F. Kennedy who once pointed out that »the line dividing domestic and foreign affairs has become as indistinct as a line drawn in water».

The history of international relations is indeed an endless catalogue of ways and means used by states to interfere in the internal affairs of other states − by force, intimidation, economic pressure, bribery or numerous more subtle methods of persuasion. The Finnish people discovered the illusion of sovereignty at the very first moment of acquiring it, when in 1918 the Western Allies withheld their recognition of Finnish independence until the country had changed its government. In 1944 again domestic politics had to be reordered to fit external circumstances. From 1948 onwards Finland's relations with the United States were greatly eased by the fact that the Communists were left out of the goverment, while the exclusion of some of the elements in the Social-Democratic and the Conservative parties was designed to reassure the Soviet Union. Time and again the Finnish people have debated, often fiercely and bitterly, to what extent considerations of foreign policy should be taken into account in decisions on domestic politics. Obviously, each situation must be judged separately. National policy cannot be a pursuit of abstract principle: »Let justice be done, though the world perish,» cannot serve as guideline for political leadership in a world ruled by power. The essential point is, however, that at all times the decision as to what course to follow has been taken by the Finns themselves, rather than imposed upon them by a foreign power. The final verdict in each situation has been given by the Finnish electorate.

What would have happened if the Finns had made different choices? Kekkonen himself has answered the question: Nothing dramatic. The Soviet government at no time attempted to impose the Communists on the Finnish people; they were not promoting a change in the Finnish system; their interest in Finland's internal affairs was defensive, not ideological. They wanted to be sure that in a clash between East and West in Europe Finland would act in accordance with the 1948

Treaty. It was no accident, as the Russians would say, that Moscow's concern about political developments in Finland coincided with tension in East-West relations. Had Kekkonen been defeated in 1962 Finnish-Soviet relations would probably have been cooled, as they did in 1948-1950. But any Finnish government would have made every effort to regain the confidence of the Soviet leaders. No one in Finland disputed the Paasikivi doctrine, according to which the best defence of Finnish independence was to convince Moscow of Finland's reliability in matters of security.

There are numerous historical precedents for the Paasikivi Line. One is described by Henry Kissinger in his early work »A World Restored» in which he writes about Metternich's efforts to win French confidence after the defeat of Austria in 1809:

»It is a policy which places a peculiar strain on the domestic principles of obligation, for it can never be legitimized by its real motives. Its success depends on its appearance of sincerity, on the ability, as Metternich once said, of seeming the dupe without being it. . . In such periods the knave and the hero, the traitor and the statesman are distinguished, not by their acts, but by their motives. . . Collaboration can be carried out successfully only by a social organism of great cohesiveness and high morale. . .»

The high degree of social cohesion that had been maintained under Paasikivi was shattered in the 1950s, not by a dispute over the substance of policy, but by a struggle for power. During the 1960s, it was gradually restored.

XIII
The Good Neighbour

After his reelection in 1968 Urho Kekkonen's leadership was accepted by all the major political parties. A man of superior intellectual capacity and the physical energy of a champion athlete, he graduated from master politician to international statesman. As memories of the power struggle of the 1950s faded, Kekkonen became a father figure to the Finnish people, the guardian of security and stability. To support Kekkonen was to support the national consensus on foreign policy, and vice versa: a perpetuum mobile of presidential power that kept Kekkonen in office for 25 years.

Kekkonen carefully cultivated his personal contacts with the Soviet leaders. Visible access to the Kremlin was his master key to power at home. Like many other men of power, Kekkonen was a firm believer in the magic of personal diplomacy. He got on specially well with Nikita Khrushchev with whom he shared a radical temperament and a robust sense of humour. But he did not let personal feelings get in the way of political interest. When told in October 1964 of Khrushchev's forced retirement and his replacement by the troika of Brezhnev, Kosygin and Podgorny, Kekkonen was visibly shaken, but recovered quickly and said: »I used to have a good friend in Moscow; I understand I now have three.» Of the three, Prime Minister Aleksei Kosygin came to replace Khrushchev as Kekkonen's closest contact in the Kremlin. Almost each year in the late 1960s and early 1970s the two men spent several days together fishing or hiking in some remote part of the Soviet Union.

The attention the Soviet leaders paid to Kekkonen clearly went beyond what could be considered normal in the case of the head of state of a small neighbouring country. I believe they looked upon him as a friendly guide to the mysterious world of Capitalism. To the members of the Soviet élite in general, Finland became a testing ground where they could safely practice the art of getting along with Westerners. It also happens to be the best shopping center in the neighbourhood.

Kekkonen on his part was able to cut through the heavy- handed Soviet bureaucracy and make quite sure the Soviet leaders understood Finnish policy on his terms. His aim was to persuade them that an independent, neutral Finland was not something they reluctantly had to tolerate, but from their own point of view a better alternative than any attempt to impose upon Finland a policy her people would regard as alien. Instead of saying no to Soviet demands he wanted Moscow to say yes to Finnish neutrality.

He succeeded with Khrushchev, but he was at all times aware of the existence of a more militant attitude on the part of those among the Soviet establishment who, like Molotov, had opposed the return of the Porkkala base and the withdrawal from Austria and who continued to criticize Khrushchev for being too soft toward the West. In autumn 1961, the divisions within the Communist camp, and apparently within the Soviet leadership itself, were brought to the surface by the Berlin crisis, with Khrushchev and his supporters arguing that in the nuclear age peaceful coexistence with the Western world had become a necessity, while the Chinese leaders and the hardliners in the Kremlin insisted that a conflict between the two camps was inevitable and all efforts had to be concentrated on preparing for it. The Soviet attitude to Finland depended on how this fundamental issue was to be resolved. To Khrushchev, neutral Finland was a showcase for the policy of peaceful coexistence he was promoting; to his opponents, Finland was merely part of the glacis in front of the ramparts along Russia's borders.

Khrushchev emerged as the winner, though at the cost of an open split with China, and even after his fall his policy with regard to Finland remained intact. But towards the end of the 1960s changes in the European situation once again affected the state of relations between Finland and the Soviet Union, though this time it was not the threat of war but rather the potential consequences of a relaxation of tensions that disturbed the Soviet leaders.

Just as Moscow was about to reach its long-standing goal of gaining Western acceptance of the existence of two German states and, in effect, of Soviet hegemony over Eastern Europe, the reform movement in Chechoslovakia − the Prague Spring − revealed what kind of forces détente was about to release within the Soviet bloc itself. The Kremlin's reponse was to close down all hatches.

With regard to Finland this meant a revision of the Chruchev position. Finnish neutrality now seemed to offer a dangerous temptation that might lead Eastern Europe astray. From 1969 on, the Soviet government became reluctant to describe Finland as a neutral country. But it was a change of doctrine, not policy. In practical terms nothing of substance changed. Most people were not even aware of any difference in Finnish-Soviet relations. Like a medieval scholastic dispute, the battle was fought between the officials who draft the sacred texts of diplomatic communiques: words words words.

The Finns did once get a glimpse of the thinking behind the words. This was in summer 1978, during a visit of the Soviet Defense Minister Dimitri Ustinov to Finland. The visit itself was nothing unusual: Soviet defense ministers have visited Finland from time to time, as have the defense ministers of the leading NATO powers. But Ustinov startled his hosts by taking up for discussion an issue that a few days before his arrival had been raised in the newspaper of the Stalinist wing of the Finnish Communist party. The paper had suggested that, since the 1948 Treaty envisages the possibility of joint action for the defense of Finnish territory, it would be useful to arrange joint Finnish-Soviet military excercises in preparation for such an eventuality.

Anyone with a reasonable understanding of Finnish policy could have told Ustinov that this would be totally unacceptable to Finland, and in fact President Kekkonen refused to enter into any discussion of the subject. As was pointed out later by the Finnish Defense Minister in reply to a parliamentary question, Finland's policy of neutrality excluded the participation of Finnish forces in joint military exercises with a foreign power.

The Finnish authorities played down the episode: after all, no formal proposal had actually been made. But the mystery lingers on. Why did Ustinov, at the time one of the most powerful men in the Kremlin, barge ahead without any advance soundings and in a manner bound to cause a leak to the press, thus putting himself in the embarassing position of receiving a public snub?

An explanation may be found through an analysis of the general trend of Soviet policy in the late 1970s. In November 1976, eighteen months before the Ustinov visit to Finland, Brezhnev visited Yugoslavia and presented Marshal Tito with a number of proposals designed to draw Yugoslavia into military cooperation with the Soviet Union. In this case, too, any competent student of international affairs could have told him his proposals would be rejected as incompatible with Yugoslavia's policy of nonalignment, and this is what in fact happened. In the following year, the Soviet Union began the deployment of SS20 missiles, with grave consequences for its relations with Western Europe. In 1978, while Ustinov was visiting Finland, Soviet garrisons were being established on three of the islands off the coast of Japan which Japan considers part of her own territory, an act that froze Soviet-Japanese relations for years to come. And a year later, at the end of 1979, the Soviet government ordered its forces to march into Afghanistan − a move that predictably caused profound damage to the political relations of the Soviet Union with both the West and leading Asian countries.

The pattern that emerges is revealing. Each of the actions I have mentioned had of course its local background and purpose. But they do have a common denominator, and that is the primacy of military objectives over political considerations in Soviet decision-making. In each case Party Leader Brezhnev appears to have listened to His Marshal's Voice. Fittingly, before his death, Brezhnev himself was elevated to the honorary rank of Soviet Marshal: a gesture symbolizing his complete identification with the militarization of Soviet foreign policy.

In this light Ustinov's behaviour in Helsinki in 1978 becomes understandable, as does Brezhnev's in Belgrade in 1976. Their purpose seems to have been to demonstrate their zeal in promoting the aspirations of the military leadership and, by doing so, to establish the line beyond which the goals of military policy could not profitably be pursued. In Finland, as in Yugoslavia, the Soviet suggestions of military cooperation, once rejected, were not mentioned again.

In Finnish-Soviet relations, 1978 marks the end of a period of roughly ten years, during which Soviet policy seems to have been influenced to a greater extent than earlier by an ambition to draw Finland closer to the Soviet bloc. Such an ambition must have existed within the military establishment as well as among the more militant elements in the Communist party. At no time did the more assertive tendency towards Finland express itself in dramatic demands or overt pressure; it was more like an undercurrent flowing below the surface of official policy. The Ustinov affair, by bringing it into the open, put an end to it. Perhaps Brezhnev told his people, in the words of Czar Nicholas I, to leave Finland alone. That is in any case what happened. After Ustinov not even a hint of any desire for change in Finnish-Soviet relations has been heard from Moscow.

The stability of the relationship survived the crucial test of the Finnish presidential election in January 1982. Kekkonen's resignation for reasons of health in October 1981 had created a sense of uncertainty and insecurity. It was feared that the consensus established under his leadership might be torn apart and the Soviet Union once again drawn into internal Finnish rivalries. Indeed, Moscow did not conceal its preference. But what happened was a triumph for the democratic process. Mauno Koivisto, the Social-Democratic candidate, received wide support across party lines and was elected by a strong majority. He had not been Moscow's favourite, but the Soviet government bowed to the will of the Finnish people and welcomed his election. It knew well that Koivisto, as all the other major candidates, was committed to continuing the foreign policy of his predecessors.

Official Finnish-Soviet encounters usually turn into ritual ceremonies of mutual reassurance. Both sides pledge allegiance to the Treaty of Friendship, Cooperation and Mutual Assistance, a rock of stability in a world in flux. Since 1948 it has been extended three times without a single change: the potential aggressor is still called »Germany» – a state that no longer can be found on the map of Europe. Like so many other treaties made in the aftermath of the Second World War, it is directed against the ghosts of the past: an agreement to prevent history from repeating itself. With the passage of time its provisions have evolved like Chinese characters – from simple pictures describing physical objects toward more abstract concepts. This does not make the Treaty less important. It has been a source of reassurance to the Soviet Union which, inspite of its enormous power, seems to suffer from a chronic sense of insecurity bred by the absence of natural or permanent borders.

The rise to power of Mikhail Gorbachev has reinforced the serenity prevailing between Finland and the Soviet Union. The new Soviet leader has repeatedly told the world his country needs »stability and predictability» in its international relations in order to devote itself to the task of modernizing the economy. Finnish-Soviet relations are a model of stability and predictability. Once again, Finland is a show case. And once again, the new Soviet leaders visit Finland to practice their skills of persuasion before venturing further into the Western world.

Like all new leaders, Gorbachev assures us that the new policies he has initiated are »irreversible». The very word invokes a healthy skepticism. But the profound technological changes to which Gorbachev is responding are indeed irreversible. When he is demanding a change from extensive to intensive methods of economic growth and a shift of emphasis from quantity to quality, he is taking the Soviet Union in a direction from which there is no turning back.

The concepts guiding Gorbachev's internal reform have a direct bearing on foreign policy. Traditionally, Russia has sought security and power by extensive means – by territorial expansion and subjugation of neighbouring nations. Driven by a deep-seated sense of insecurity, Russia has pursued for centuries what has been called an »insatiable« defensive policy. But today the extensive method is out of date, not only in economic development but also in the search for security. Acquisition of territory no longer brings defensive advantage. Keeping subordinate nations under control in the imperial manner places an increasing strain on central authority. The »zone of security« created in Eastern and Central Europe has become a zone of vulnerability. Afghanistan, in the words of Gorbachev himself, is a »bleeding wound«. The gigantic military machine built up during the Brezhnev era to enable the Soviet Union to keep up with the United States as a global super power has drained the Soviet system of vitality. Gorbachev's ambitious plan of modernizing the Soviet Union cannot succeed unless he can curb the atavistic territorial instinct of the Russian nation.

The case of Finland is instructive. The strip of land conquered by the Soviet Union in 1944 at great cost has been useless for Soviet security. Instead, the political relationship between the two countries, based as it is on respect for the right of the Finnish people to choose their own way of life, has provided Moscow with a friendly neighbour and a useful trading partner. Finland today is usually described by the Soviet leaders as »a good neighbour«, and this is not just a polite phrase. Do they have another?

XIV
The Finnish Paradox

The ups and downs in Finnish-Soviet relations have been reflected, sometimes as if by a distorting mirror, in changes in Western attitudes to Finland. Having written off Finland after the Second World War as lost to Communism, Western opinion at first regarded the Finnish claim of neutrality with the embarrassed disbelief with which families sometimes greet the return of a soldier who has been reported missing in battle and presumed dead. Since Finland prudently plays down differences with the Soviet Union, she has had difficulties in proving her indentity. Kekkonen once tried to explain the »Finnish paradox», as he called it, as follows:

»Normally it would seem that when in a border country between West and East the influence of the Western world is on the increase, the influence of the East would correspondingly diminish. And in reverse, if the influence of the Eastern world grows, the West must retreat. Finland is one of the countries on the border of West and East. But in our case, the better we succeed in maintaining the confidence of the Soviet Union in Finland as a peaceful neighbour, the better are our possibilities for close cooperation with the countries of the Western world. . .»

This was too subtle to be grasped by commentators who tend to apply a sort of decibel test to Finnish policy: the louder Finland condemns the Soviet Union, the greater is her independence. But the Finnish paradox has been understood and accepted by the governments of the Western powers which from the early 1960s onward have consistently recognized the neutrality of Finland and pledged their respect for it. Neutrality is, after all, the best deal the West can get out of Finland.

As relations between East and West began to improve, it was assumed both sides would finally overcome any reservations they might have about Finnish neutrality. In fact, however, the Finnish paradox appeared in a new light. On both sides détente was perceived as a threat to the cohesion within the respective alliances. Just as towards the end of the 1960s Moscow grew uneasy about the possible implications of Finnish neutrality for Eastern Europe, so on the Western side critics of détente feared the Finnish example might seduce West European nations into imagining that it could be possible to live in peace with the Soviet Union without the protection of a strong military alliance. In West Germany, Franz-Josef Strauss launched the term of »Finlandisation» into the political debate, and it has stayed in orbit ever since.

Finlandisation is defined as a process by which a democratic nation living in the shadow of the military superiority of a totalitarian power is forced to submit to the political domination of that power and finally looses its internal freedom. This, of course, is just the opposite of what actually has happened to Finland, a country that today enjoys a much greater freedom of action than anyone could have imagined forty years ago. But Finlandisation never was addressed to Finland herself. It is not a description of historical reality but a warning of the fate awaiting the nations of Western Europe if they were foolish enough to trust the Russians and lower their guard. As has been explained by the French writer Alain Minc in his book Le Syndrome Finlandais (1986), Finland has been able to maintain her freedom because she can lean on the West, but Western Europe, if abandoned by the United States, would have no choice but to submit to Soviet blackmail. In his view the hedonistic, overprotected societies of Western Europe, inspite of their great wealth and potential collective power, would simply lack the will to organize their defense on a scale that would maintain the balance of power in Europe. Put in this way, the fear of Finlandisation is yet another symptom of the bleeding inferiority complex which is sapping the self-confidence of Western Europe.

The fact remains, however, that the term is used to discredit the policy of Finland. The charge is that Finland adjusts her internal politics in anticipation of Soviet wishes, avoids antagonizing Moscow by refraining from open criticism of Soviet violations of international law or human rights, turns back political refugees crossing the Finnish border from Russia, and practises a humiliating degree self- censorship. In sum, the freedom of Finland is a mere illusion, like a play performed on a stage with the Soviets controlling the lights.

True enough, Finnish policy is designed to avoid antagonizing Moscow. Actually, Finnish policy is designed to avoid antagonizing any important power: surely the course of wisdom for a small neutral nation heavily dependent on foreign trade. During the Vietnam war, for instance, Finnish criticism of United States actions was muted, as was gratefully noted in Washington. The Soviet invasions of Hungary and Chechoslovakia were passionately denounced by large crowds demonstrating in the streets of Helsinki, but in the United Nations the Finnish delegation coolly abstained from voting in favour of resolutions condemning the Soviet actions, remembering the advice of J.W. Snellman who a hundred years earlier had warned his countrymen against indulging in the luxury of making self-satisfying gestures which could only harm Finland herself without helping the victims of aggression.

It would be foolish to claim that the Finnish performance over the past decades has been flawless. To use a phrase from Kissinger's analysis of the policy of Metternich I have quoted earlier, there are both »dupes and knaves» among Finnish politicians. There have been lapses from the strict application of neutrality in the disputes between the great powers. There is an inclination to use a double standard in judging international events. But the validity of a political concept is not nullified by human failing in its execution.

The Finnish policy of restraint is often taken to reveal a limitation of sovereignty, an abdication from the pursuit of the national interest. It is, of course, the very opposite: an expression of the »sacro egoismo» of the nation, a rejection of the claims of ideological solidarity. Those who complain about Finland's lack of engagement in promoting freedom and human rights in the Soviet Union fail to understand that the Finns have strong reasons of their own to adhere to the strict classical interpretation of the principle of non-interference in the internal affairs of other states. Apart from principle, Finns tend to be skeptical about Western hopes of promoting change in the Soviet Union. On the whole, Finns believe they can see behind the facade of Soviet ideology the familiar features of Mother Russia, a power not easily moved by outside exhortation.

The sacro egoismo of the Finnish people is crystallized in their attitude to refugees. In contrast to Sweden where the number of immigrants and their children is more than one tenth of the total population, Finland remains a closed society. The number of residents who are not Finnish citizens is less than 20 000.

Job seekers from the Third World are turned away. The few Soviet citizens who manage to evade the Soviet frontier guards and slip across the border are carefully screened by the Finnish authorities. It is not true, as is widely believed, that all are sent back. Political asylum is granted to those who are judged to be genuine political refugees. But such cases are not publicized, and the policy in general is to discourage any notion that Finnish territory might serve as a comfortable escape route from the Soviet Union.

From time to time the handling of individual cases has been criticized, but there can be no doubt that the policy itself enjoys solid popular support. The same can be said of restricting immigration from the Third World. A few liberal- minded politicians have begun to speak of Finland's duty, in the name of international solidarity, to let more people in, and the present immigration quota of 200 persons a year may well be increased. But in the foreseeable future Finland is likely to remain a homogeneous nation with only tiny racial or other minorities. Intellectuals complain of the lack of stimulating cultural diversity, but the vast majority of Finns congratulate themselves on having avoided the social and racial strife that has spread throughout the rest of Western Europe in the wake of large-scale immigration. Rightly or wrongly, the absence of terrorism, the relatively low degree of street violence and drug abuse, even the small number of AIDS cases are counted among the blessings.

At heart, the Finnish attitude to immigrants, including those who try to escape from the Soviet Union, is dictated by the mechanisms of self-preservation developed over centuries in response to external pressures. The issue of self-censorship, too, must be examined in the context of the Finnish tradition.

Somehow Finland has become labelled the country

of self- censorship, as if it were a Finnish invention unknown to other democracies. In fact, of course, self-censorship is practiced in every society where there is no official censor telling editors what they may or may not publish. Freedom of the press makes every editor his own censor: he himself must decide, to quote the masthead of the New York Times, what is or is not »fit to print». The criteria vary from country to country and change with the times. In time of war or manifest external danger it is taken for granted that a responsible paper will refuse to publish material that might cause damage to national security, endanger the success of sensitive negotiations with a foreign government, provoke an adversary or offend an ally. In peaceful conditions an editor will feel less inhibited, but at no time can he completely disregard the possible effect his decisions may have on the national interest.

What happens when, for instance, an important state visit is in danger of being spoilt by the showing of a TV programme likely to offend the distinguished visitor? The Prime Minister calls the director of the broadcasting company and asks him to withdraw the programme, and the director, being a patriotic man, agrees to do it. This is what happened in Britain when the King of Saudi Arabia was about to arrive and Prime Minister Margaret Thatcher discovered the BBC was about to broadcast a documentary about violations of human rights in the visitor's country. Had a similar incident happened in Finland it would have been held up by the world's press as an example of self- censorship.

One such example often cited is what happened to Solzhenitsyn's book on the Gulag in Finland. His regular Finnish publisher, a small house with links to the Social- Democratic party, decided to back out so as not to embarrass its political patrons. The news of this was flashed around the world as proof of Finnish subservience to the Soviet Union. Actually another publisher stepped in, and all the volumes of Solzhenitsyn's work were published in Finnish. But this was no longer news. Nor did anyone recall the difficulty George Orwell had in finding a British publisher prepared to risk offending the Russians by publishing Animal Farm. But at that time, of course, the Soviet Union was an ally of Britain.

Self-censorship is not unknown to Americans either. In February 1987 a fictional TV series describing life in Soviet occupied America stirred up a lively debate about its possible effect on American-Soviet relations. Several distinguished columnists expressed the view that the programme was harmful to the interests of the United States and should not have been shown. No one, of course, actually used the word self-censorship, but that is what the critics of the programme in effect advocated.

If it is even remotely possible that a miniseries on television might damage the foreign policy interests of a super power, then the media in a small nation like Finland ought to be careful indeed. In the period immediately after the Second World War the Finnish press did in fact exercise great caution in dealing with material relating to the Soviet Union, in support of the government's effort to gain the trust of the Soviet leaders. Such loyalty to the national cause was in keeping with the traditions of the Finnish press. During the war and in the period preceeding it similar discretion was common in dealing with Germany. The American concept of the role of the press as a permanent adversary to authority is alien to Finland. The Finnish press performs its function, which is of course to inform and criticize, within the national consensus, not in opposition to it.

As Finland's international position has become more stable and secure, editorial judgment as to what is or is not fit to print has become more relaxed. If those who repeat the charge that the Finnish media dare not tell the truth about the Soviet Union would take the trouble to examine a Finnish newspaper, they would find that the coverage of international affairs, including the Soviet Union, today is indistinguishable in all essentials from that of the press in any Western country. Even the most suspicious foreign critic would be hard put to finding traces of what could be called self-censorship. Altogether, the media in Finland are becoming »Americanized»: more critical of those in power, more commercial, more ruthless in the pursuit of revelations, much less inclined to accept the government's view of the national interest. The trend is inevitable. The risk is, however, that it may erode Finland's ability to conduct a rational and consistent foreign policy. A reasonable degree of self-censorship is a necessary element in the defensive mechanism of a small neutral nation.

XV
The Crucial Test

The ultimate purpose of Finland's policy of neutrality is to keep the country out of war. Since a local, isolated attack against Finland can be ruled out, her chances of success must be judged in the context of a general European conflict. The crucial test will be the credibility of Finnish policy at a moment of supreme tension, when both sides believe war is imminent and make their moves accordingly.

The question often asked is how a country bound to the Soviet Union by a treaty of mutual assistance can hope to remain neutral in such a situation. The answer is, as I have pointed out earlier, that the 1948 Treaty contains no provisions that could prevent Finland from staying neutral. Military cooperation with the Soviet Union is envisaged only in the event that neutrality has failed and Finnish territory has been attacked from the West. Even then responsibility for the defence of Finland will rest primarily with the Finns themselves and Soviet assisttance will be given only if needed.

The scenario sketched out in the relevant articles of the Treaty comes to life in a historical perspective. Twice in his lifetime Stalin had seen German troops marching through Finland against Russia. In 1948 he was obsessed with the danger of a revival of German power, and he was determined to make sure the Finns would not again join Russia's enemies or let them through without resistance.

Such explanations are usually brushed aside as so-

An example of modern Finnish architecture: a church in a suburb of Helsinki, designed by Juha Leiviskä. (Lehtikuva)

A Finnish landscape: forest and lakes. (Lehtikuva)

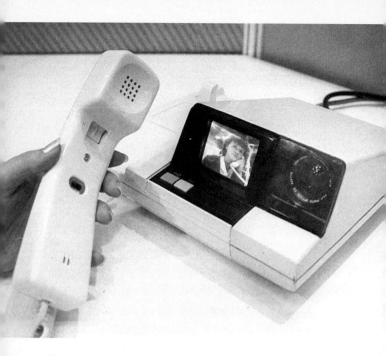

Europe's first videophone was developed in Finland. (Pressfoto)

The world's biggest industrial robot built by the Finnish firm Tammec is used for welding at the Wärtsilä shipyard in Helsinki. (Lehtikuva)

Luxury cruise ships are another speciality of Finnish shipyards. (Lehtikuva)

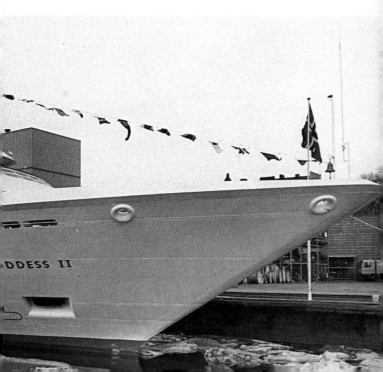

phistry. Surely, it is said, the Soviet leaders will not let themselves be hobbled by legal niceties. In a critical situation they will do whatever they think is necessary, regardless of what is written in the Finnish-Soviet Treaty.

So it is not, after all, the Treaty which in this view would prevent Finland from staying neutral. The Treaty, on the contrary, if observed as it is written, reinforces Finland's policy of neutrality. But the Treaty, according to the skeptics, would be ignored. The Russians would come anyway.

This view is based on two assumption, the validity of which is usually held to be self-evident. One is that in a critical situation Finland will be a mere object of Soviet policy, with no power to influence the course of events. The other assumption is that it can be taken for granted the Soviet Union would want to move its own forces forward into Finnish territory. Both assumptions need critical examination.

On the first point, the record of the past fifty years tells a different story. Time and again Finland has been able to assert her own interests in critical situations. In 1944, her resistance converted the demand for surrender into a negotiated settlement. In 1948, the treaty model offered by Stalin was rejected by Finland. In 1961, Kekkonen persuaded Chruchev to drop his proposal for military consultations. In 1978, Ustinov was rebuffed.

The second assumption, too, should be examined against the historical record. In 1944, at a time when Finland still was an enemy country, Stalin insisted that the German army remaining in Lapland must be driven out by Finnish forces without Soviet assistance. The explanation was simple: he needed all the divisions he could muster elsewhere, for far more important tasks. Strategically Finland was a side issue.

Oil drilling equipment produced in Finland. (Lehtikuva)

The same is likely to be the case in a future global conflict. The military capabilities of the Soviet Union, vast as they are, will be stretched to their utmost. Finland will be one of the less important sectors. The Soviet leaders might well prefer to leave the defence of Finnish territory to the Finns themselves, especially if the alternative of going in uninvited would be seen to lead to a confrontation with a hostile population.

Finland's policy is designed to convince Moscow that it is in the Soviet interest to leave the job of defending Finland to the Finns themselves. Accordingly, the primary task of Finland's armed forces is to mount a credible defence against a possible attempt by Nato forces to cross Finnish territory, by land or by air, in an attack against the Soviet Union.

But what would Finland do in the event of an aggressive move by Soviet forces across Finnish territory into Sweden or Norway? Naturally enough this is the question asked in the West.

It was answered by President Kekkonen when, in 1965, he assured Finland's Western neighbours, Norway in particular, that Finland was not committed by treaty to join an aggression and would not permit any other country to use Finnish territory for an aggressive purpose. Yet doubts persisted, and in January 1983 General Bernard Rogers, then Supreme Commander of Nato forces in Europe, questioned at a press conference the willingness of the Finnish people to defend their country. His remarks revealed a disturbing ignorance, not just about Finland but more generally about the behaviour of nations in time of danger. The reaction in Finland was indignant. But the general unwittingly did the Finns a service. The debate his comment caused cleared the air. The doubts he had brought into the open have been largely dispelled. Since then high Western defence officials have spoken respectfully of

Finland's defence effort; among them Admiral Crowe who visited Finland in 1986 as Chairman of the Joint Chiefs of Staff of the United States.

About the will of the Finnish people there can be no doubt. In an international opinion poll conducted in several Western countries young men of military age were asked two questions: Were they willing to defend their country should war break out and did they believe in the ability of the armed forces to defend their country? On both questions the percentage of those answering yes was highest in Finland.

This is not really suprising. The response to questions of this kind is not a product of intellectual analysis: it is a gut reaction. The attitude of the present generation grows out of the collective memory of the national experience. Finland, alone among the nations of the European continent, defended herself successfully in the last war, the country was not humiliated and occupied: this is the source of present self-confidence.

The results of the international poll should be read in conjunction with those of Finnish national polls. These reveal a near unanimity on defence issues: More than 90 percent approve of the way foreign policy has been conducted, close to 90 percent agree the country should be defended even if the outcome is uncertain, and more than 80 percent believe the Finnish-Soviet Treaty of 1948 has a positive effect on Finland's international position.

The message of the polls is reinforced by the Finnish record of military service. Conscription has been maintained ever since Finland became independent. Annually more than 90 percent of the young men liable to military service actually enter the armed forces. This is one of the highest percentages in the world. It has provided Finland with trained reserves of up to 700 000 men, of whom some 44 000 take part in annual refresher courses. Over 200 000 of these reserves, supported by regulars, comprise a »fast deployment force» that could be mobilized within 48 hours.

The proportion of officers, both in active Service and in the reserve, is higher than in any other Western country. The number of conscripts applying for reserve officer training, which means longer service, regularly exceeds the capacity of the training facilities. Altogether, the social standing and prestige of the armed forces remain high. Pacifist tendencies are less prominent than in the other Nordic countries or indeed in Western Europe as a whole.

The will is there, but what about the means?

The peace treaty imposed upon Finland by the Allied Powers in 1947 places a number of constraints on her defence forces. But even within the prescribed limits the material resources available to the defence forces remain modest. Defence spending as a proportion of GNP is officially less than two percent, but if defence-related items not included in the defence budget are counted, the real figure is just above that level. This is a lower proportion than in other European countries, with the exception of Austria.

In assessing the cost-effectiveness of Finland's defence policy two factors should be kept in mind. One is geography. In contrast to most European states, Finland can be defended by relatively low-cost ground forces. The army is organized for what is called territorial defence, which is a polite term for guerilla warfare. Nature and climate help to make Finland an exceedingly uncomfortable place for uninvited guests.

The second point is that Finland pampers her soldiers less than most West-European countries. If they were paid at the same rate as for instance Danish troops, another 25 per cent would have to be added to the defence budget. As it is, an important proportion, up to one third, can be devoted to procurement of materiel.

During the first half of the 1980s military spending was steadily increased. The defence of Lapland received special attention. As a result, Finland today maintains ground forces in the Far North equal to those of Sweden and Norway, thus demonstrating her determination to maintain control of the sensitive area in the vicinity of the Soviet base on the Kola peninsula.

The Soviet military build-up on Kola is of course not directed against the Nordic countries. As a basing area for the Soviet strategic submarine force and the Northern Fleet, Kola has a vital role in maintaining the strategic nuclear balance between the two super powers. But inevitably it casts a shadow over the northern parts of Finland, Sweden and Norway.

The Soviet need to protect the base is obvious. At the same time the growing power of the Soviet Northern Fleet poses a threat to the sealines of communication linking the United States to Europe. Nato is responding to the challenge by intensifying its maritime and other military activities in the area. Northern Norway has become one of the most sensitive neuralgic points in the strategic plans of both military alliances.

The image of the Nordic region as a placid backwater in world politics has thus been shattered. In case of war, there would be an obvious danger of military operations around northern Norway spilling over to the territories of the two neutrals, Finland or Sweden. Yet military analysts tend to overdramatize the change in the Nordic situation. True, the military activity of both alliances in the area has increased considerably in the past ten to fifteen years. But so it has in several other parts of the world. In the Pacific basin, for instance, the increase surely has been proportionately much greater than in the Nordic region. The militarization of the policies of both super powers has been global in scope, and the Nordic area has received its due share of the consequences. But the subtle collusion between the Soviet Union and Norway designed to minimize political tension is reassuring. Inspite of the military build-up, the Nordic area remains politically peaceful and stable: this is not where war might begin.

Yet the geopolitical split dividing the Nordic nations remains. The Norwegians cannot imagine their country could stay out of a war between Nato and the Warsaw Pact. Nor can the Danes, gatekeepers of the Baltic. The Finns and the Swedes do believe they might succeed, though the latter's faith has been somewhat shaken by Soviet naval activities in their waters.

There is, however, one thing that unites the Nordic countries in the field of defence: none of them has nuclear weapons on its territory. The Nordic region is the only large nuclear-free area comprising several states, both Nato members and neutral, in Europe. It is likely to remain so. True, the Nordic governments have been unable to agree on a treaty formalizing the nuclear-free status of their countries: on making the zone a Zone. Norway and Denmark insist on keeping their »nuclear option» for use in time of war or crisis. But it is increasingly unlikely that nuclear weapons would actually ever be deployed on Norwegian or Danish soil.

In this respect conditions have changed fundamentally since the early 1960s, when President Kekkonen first proposed the creation of a Nordic nuclear-free zone. At that time the Swedish government had not yet made up its mind on whether or not to produce its own nuclear weapons, while Nato's »flexible response» was believed to require the use of Danish or Norwegian bases by bombers carrying nuclear weapons. Kekkonen's primary purpose was to make clear that Finland in no circumstances would accept nuclear weapons to be deployed on her territory.

Since then Sweden has given up her nuclear option, and technology has rendered the Danish and Norwegian bases obsolete. The two countries can be defended by nuclear weapons from outside their territories. But the nuclear option has acquired a symbolic value. It is like an oath of allegiance to Nato. Thus the debate about the Zone in the Nordic area is not so much about the defence of the area itself as about Nato's nuclear policy in general. Those who oppose a nuclear-free Zone fear the spread of »nuclear allergy» to other Nato countries; those who advocate a Zone wish to promote a shift of Nato policy away from reliance on the first use of nuclear weapons.

A nuclear-free zone cannot guarantee immunity from nuclear attack. But so long as it has no nuclear weapons on its territory a country may have a chance of avoiding the penalty of becoming a direct target for the nuclear strikes of the other side, while having nuclear weapons on one's own territory is virtually certain to bring with it that penalty. For a small nation this could be literally fatal. When national survival is at stake, limiting the danger of being involved in a nuclear war becomes the overriding purpose of policy.

The nuclear dilemma is bound to erode solidarity within the military alliances − on both sides, but of course more visibly in Nato. The purpose of the alliances is twofold: to deter aggression and, failing that, provide effective defence. Everyone still wants deterrence to function, but a growing opinion in Europe rejects a defence based on the use of nuclear weapons − and yet fails to support spending more money on conventional defence.

The neutral nations of Europe are able to evade this dilemma, although obviously they, too, are affected by how it will be resolved. Neutrality is in essence a policy of having your cake and eating it too.

Leaving aside the variety of policies of nonalignment in the Third World, neutrality in the classical sense can be practiced only in a relatively stable international environment based on a balance of power between two or more groups of states. Since in a Europe dominated by one power neutrality would become untenable or irrelevant, the neutrals are often accused of getting a free ride by hitching their security to the balance of power paid for by the members of the alliances. In fact, however, neither alliance has any interest in seeking to convert or absorb the neutral states in Europe.

In the case of Finland, the way she was able to close her »missile gap» casts light on how her policy of neutrality is viewed by the two alliances.

The problem was that the Finnish Peace Treaty of 1947 prohibits the possession of »self-propelled or guided missiles or projectiles». At the time the Treaty was drafted the phrase was meant to cover such offensive weapons as the V-1 and V-2 missiles used by the Germans during the Second World War. By the end of the 1950s, however, the family of missiles had multiplied to the extent that its members had become to dominate virtually all aspects of military activity. Far from remaining exclusively offensive weapons, guided missiles had become indispensable for defence. Without air-to-air missiles fired by fighter planes or ground-to-air anti-aircraft missiles no country could defend its airspace against hostile aircraft.

For Finland the lack of missiles presented an intolerable problem. The preservation of neutrality required the creation of an effective air defence. The other countries with similar peace treaties, Italy, Bulgaria, Rumania and Hungary, all members of military alliances, had simply ignored the limitations imposed upon their armed forces and acquired whatever weapons they considered necessary. But this could not be the Finnish way. A cardinal principle of Finnish foreign policy is strict adherence to treaty obligations. Yet the idea of revising the Treaty by agreement between the signatories was not realistic either. Neither the Soviet Union nor the Western powers were prepared to risk opening what they feared to be a Pandora's box of complaints and claims from other countries.

Finally an ingenuous way out was found. The Finnish government persuaded the other signatories, principally the Soviet Union on the one side and Britain acting with the consent of the United States on the other, to agree to a »re-interpretation» of the relevant Particle of the Peace Treaty permitting Finland to acquire missiles for defensive purposes. This, it was argued, could not be contrary to the spirit and the purpose of the Treaty. Its military provisions were designed to prevent Finland from developing an offensive military capability, but not to deprive her of her right to self-defense.

Having obtained the consent of all the signatories at the end of 1962, Finland quickly consummated the agreement by buying missiles from both the Soviet Union and Britain. She continues to maintain a rough balance between purchases of war materiel from East and West. The Finnish air force, for instance, flies Swedish Drakens and Soviet Migs as well as British Hawks.

The agreement to re-interpret the Peace Treaty without actually revising it remains a unique case in the history of diplomacy. Austrian attempts to use the same device to get around a similar provision in her State Treaty have been rebuffed by the Soviet Union.

Arms sales usually carry a political message. By agreeing to sell her fighters and missiles both alliances implicitly show confidence in Finland's determination to defend her neutrality and willingness to respect it in time of war.

XVI
The Moral Dimension

Finnish officers and troops keeping the peace under the blue flag of the United Nations in far-away places like the Golan Hights or Lebanon or Kashmir represent the moral dimension of neutrality. Like the other neutrals, Finland works hard at convincing the world that her policy is not merely a way of saving her own skin, but actually serves the higher interests of the international community. A neutral country is able to provide such useful services as mediation or peace-keeping forces, and it can make out-of-the-way meeting places available to the leaders of the big powers. By making itself useful a neutral country reinforces its own neutrality. When pressed to support one side against the other, it can take refuge behind the argument that taking sides would impair its usefulness. Thus, like Narcissus, a neutral country draws strength from its own image. Each hopes to be recognized as another Switzerland marked by a protective Red Cross on the maps of the strategists of the big powers.

In the past quarter-century, Finland has contributed officers or troops to every peace-keeping operation mounted by the United Nations and maintains permanent stand-by forces so as to be able to respond promptly to a UN request for peace-keeping services. The other Nordic countries have made similar arrangements. In the UN, where European security issues are seldom discussed, the Nordic countries work in close unity. This privileged little group of politically stable, socially advanced, prosperous countries which have no major international claims to press or to counter, no present or recent colonial record, and no racial problems, represents moderation and rationality in an assembly often swayed by fanatic or neurotic forces. In acting as »model members of the UN», as U Thant once called them, the Nordic nations go beyond mere image-making: they have every reason, in their own interest, to work for the peaceful settlement of international disputes and thus reduce the risks of a general conflict.

The Nordic vision of a rational world order was personified in Dag Hammarskjöld as Secretary-General of the United Nations. He is not widely remembered today. I believe, however, that his extraordinary effort to play an autonomous role in world politics – an effort that ended in political failure and personal tragedy – carries a lesson which still is relevant.

How Hammarskjöld came to be appointed Secretary-General in 1952 is a story abounding in irony. He did not seek the office, and those who selected him had no intention of launching him onto a spectacular career. The big powers at the time were tired of the political pretensions of Tryggve Lie, the first Secretary- General; they wanted a faceless bureaucrat to run the Secretariat and Dag Hammarskjöld, a neutral civil servant from neutral Sweden, seemed perfect for the part.

For a while Hammarskjöld did concentrate, as was expected of him, on his administrative duties. But in 1955 his successful initiative in negotiating the release of American airmen captured in China gave him a first taste of independent political action, and the Suez crisis in 1956 propelled him into the centre of the world stage. On his reappointment to a second term in 1957, Hammarskjöld was ready to put forward a revolutionary concept of the role of the Secretary-General. In his view, the Secretary-General should act independently, even in the absence of any decisions of the main organs of the United Nations, to fill any »vacuum» created by the failure of the powers to agree on issues affecting world peace. Since he had no means of power at his disposal, he had to rely on such innovative devices as the UN peace-keeping force in the Suez, observers in Lebanon and a »presence» in Laos.

For a few moments in history the Secretary-General did become an autonomous influence in international politics, an influence not based on power but representing, in Hammarskjöld's words, »the detached element in international life». He claimed the UN was »the main protector of the interests of those many nations who feel themselves strong as members of the international family but who are weak in isolation». In his famous rebuttal of Chruchev's charges of partiality, Hammarskjöld pointed out that it was not the Soviet Union or any other big power who needed the United Nations for their protection, but »all the others». To the new states emerging from colonial rule Hammarskjöld offered the services of the UN as a shield against the predatory designs of the two rival blocs.

Hammarskjöld's last year at the UN can now be seen as an effort to transform the Organization from an organ of co- operation between sovereign states into an instrument of the collective responsibility of the membership: a heroic effort doomed to failure. True, a convincing case can be made to prove that, on balance, Hammarskjöld maintained impartiality between West and East. But it was a mistake to believe that the governments of the big powers would judge him by some abstract or objective criteria. Chruchev or de Gaulle was not likely to say to himself, »This time Hammarskjöld went against us, but it is only fair, last time he was with us.» They judged him by the political consequences of his actions in each concrete case separately. When his actions in the Congo went against Soviet interests, Moscow turned on him, and it did not help him that France, Belgium and Britain were also dissatisfied with what he was doing there. The big powers were prepared to support him only so long as both sides in the Cold War could benefit from what he did. They would not tolerate a policy equally damaging to both sides. United Nations was never meant to limit the freedom of action of its principal founding members.

The lesson of Hammarskjöld's failure was clear. The United Nations cannot be turned into an Association for the Prevention of Cruelty to Small Nations. The realities of power prevail within the Organization as they do outside. Without a minimum degree of cooperation between the big powers the UN simply does not work. The small nations cannot win by ganging up against the big ones; instead they must try to persuade the big powers to cooperate and make use of UN services.

In the latter part of the 1960s the superpowers did take steps in that direction. Détente between the United States and the Soviet Union softened the sharp edges of earlier confrontations. The Soviet leaders were obsessed with what they perceived to be a deadly threat from Mao's China and were seeking tacit American support against her. Americans were preoccupied with the war in Vietnam and they, too, believed China to be the main obstacle to peace.

A common enemy is a powerful bond. Americans and Russians began to look upon the United Nations as a forum of co- operation. The Organization offered ready-made facilities for the joint management of conflicts and crises in the Third World. In 1967, the Security Council unanimously adopted its famous Resolution 242 designed to bring about a comprehensive settlement of the Middle-East conflict: probably the high point so far in the use of the UN as an instrument for the maintenance of international peace and security. A year later, the United States and the Soviet Union brought to the United Nations for approval the treaty to prevent the spread of nuclear weapons and offered special security guarantees to nations which, by adhering to the treaty, might expose themselves to a threat from a nuclear power: though none was named, only one − China − could be meant. And in 1973, the two superpowers once again found they needed UN services to help them pacify the Middle- East.

Among the small nations all this raised hopes of a more constructive role for the UN, but also the usual fear of a superpower condominium. The divergence between the reactions of Finland and Sweden was revealing. The Swedes, sure of their neutral status, declared a plague on both houses, while Finland used the opportunity to earn credit with both superpowers by placing herself at their disposal.

But superpower harmony in the United Nations did not last long. After the entry of the representatives of the Peking government in 1971, Chinese-Soviet rivalry for the support of the Third World countries inhibited Moscow from further collusion with imperialist America. The oil crisis in 1973 let loose in the United Nations a wave of aggressive radicalism which alienated American opinion. The end of détente finally paralyzed the UN. By the end ofthe 1970s the UN had lost much of its importance even as the primary forum for negotiations between the rich and the poor nations. The Western world was turning its back on it: This was the deadliest weapon − indifference.

There is a sharp paradox in the decline of the world's

first universal organization at a time of growing inter-dependence between nations. The consequences of modern technology flow across national boundaries creating problems that cry out for global action. Yet the internationalist ideology that inspired the founding fathers of the United Nations has lost its vitality, and the belief in the essential unity of mankind and the validity of universal values has been weakened by particularism of every kind.

In a world divided by diverse and conflicting beliefs and interests any attempt to reform or reconstruct the UN would be doomed to fail. What prevents member states from using the Organization is the lack of political will rather than any fault in its mechanisms. The moment the will is there the way to use UN services will be found, as experience has shown. And sooner or later — probably sooner rather than later — the superpowers will discover once again that they need these services.

But first the UN system itself must be saved. The decision of the Unites States to withdraw from UNESCO was a danger signal that had a salutary effect. In 1986 the United Nations Assembly finally initiated a financial and administrative clean-up of the Organization. This is a necessary first step toward restoring confidence in the UN.

Together with the other Nordic states, Finland has been in the vanguard of this rescue action. Support for the UN remains a centre piece of Finnish foreign policy. The vision of an international order based on the UN Charter continues to provide the cloak of idealism every nation needs to wrap around itself on solemn occasions: If only all the others behaved as well as we do! In practical terms, however, the focus of Finnish foreign policy has shifted away from the global abstractions of the UN to the realities of Europe — a region where the prospects of change offer both opportunity and risk.

XVII
The Message of Helsinki

As the site of the signing in August 1975 of the Final Act of the Conference on Security and Co-operation in Europe (CSCE), Helsinki has joined the list of place names which are used in the international debate like shorthand symbols to denote important turning points in the affairs of nations. But the meaning of Helsinki continues to arouse intense controvercy.

The Finns have their own parochial view. In their eyes the gathering in their capital of thirtyfive heads of state or government was the grand finale of Finland's long labours to gain international recognition of her status as a neutral country. Finnish neutrality, as President Kekkonen noted, was thus firmly embedded into the European structure.

On the more general significance of Helsinki interpretations vary widely. In the Soviet view, Helsinki stands for the immutability of the European system that emerged from the Second World War. In the official Western view, it is a promise of change – change, that is, on the other side of the dividing line between East and West – and this view is shared by many people on that side, a few of whom have dared voice it publicly. And then there are those who dismiss the CESC as a show without substance, mere figure skating on the hard surface of reality, designed to lull the West into lowering its guard and so to weaken the real foundation for peace and security – the balance of military power.

The title of the conference − Security and Co- operation in Europe − is deceptively simple. In fact every word is riddled with ambiguity. What for instance is meant by Europe? In the context of security, Europe must be defined in geopolitical rather than geographical terms. At the insistence of Western Europe, the United States and Canada were included from the outset: at least something had been learned from history.

But one European country was missing. Of all the states invited, and they included the Vatican, San Marino and Lichtenstein, the only one to say no was Albania, at the time China's European spokesman. The Chinese scornfully labelled Helsinki a »conference of insecurity», a plot by the two superpowers to keep the smaller nations under control. Insecurity perhaps for China herself whose leaders in those days feared the Soviet Union was planning to secure its Western front in order to be free to turn eastward. Today, this fear appears to have faded. Still, geopolitical Europe stops at the Urals, as General de Gaulle first defined it.

Security, too, is an elusive term. There are no objective criteria acceptable to all. Traditionally states have sought security at the expense of other states or through withdrawal into fortified isolation. Lebensraum was supposed to bring security to the German people, and the Maginot Line to the French. In fact twice in this century the competitive search for security has laid waste the greater part of Europe. Technology has now at last convinced the Europeans that neither territorial gain nor elaborate fortifications can bring security. Yet the Helsinki Conference made no attempt to construct a collective security system to replace the system of alliances. European security, it was taken for granted in Helsinki, would continue to rest on MAD − Mutual Assured Destruction − as an

effective deterrent against war between the two alliances. The more modest goal of the CSCE was to make
life in the shadow of the balance of terror less dangerous.

Thus the Helsinki Conference differed fundamentally from previous attempts to create a stable European order. The Congress of Vienna in 1815 sought
to restore the world as it had been before the Na-
poleonic wars: legitimacy was its guiding principle. The
Holy Alliance formed to maintain the order created in
Vienna did not stop war, either in Europe or even less
in other continents, but the basic structure of Europe
did remain intact for a hundred years, until shattered
in the First World War. At Versailles, a new guiding
principle was introduced - national self- determination.
The Austro-Hungarian Empire was carved up, and the
Russian Empire dismembered. But the collective security system of the League of Nations broke down
within two decades. In Helsinki, the organizing principle was ostensibly ideology, in that the division of the
continent into two ideological systems was implicitly
recognized. But in actual fact it is not ideology that
divides the European peoples: the ideological barriers
are propped up by the armies. Ideology in today's Europe grows out of the barrel of the gun: it is a function
of military power. This, then, is the true guiding principle of the present order: recognition of the facts of
power.

The Soviet objective in proposing the security conference was clear. It was to serve as a substitute for the
peace conference that never was held after the Second
World War. The purpose was to legitimize the territorial and political changes brought about by the war:
the fruits of the Soviet victory. The West was asked
to ratify the Soviet version of the Monroe Doctrine.
This is, of course, what was meant by recognition of

the status quo in Europe, the phrase most commonly used to describe the purpose of the Helsinki Conference. Explicit acceptance of things as they are was esssential, in the Soviet view, to ensure peace in Europe. Ambiguity in the Western attitude to the frontiers or the regimes in Eastern Europe kept alive hopes of change which in turn bred insecurity. The dangerous consequences had been seen in Hungary in 1956 and in Czechoslovakia in 1968. Stability was the key to peace and security, and to cooperation between East and West.

The West has had neither the will nor the means to challence the Soviet concept of security. But it did succeed in Helsinki to write into the Final Act its own concept which rejects the notion that security must for ever rest on the harsh and unnatural separation of the European peoples between East and West. True security, in the Western view, must be based on genuine mutual confidence, and such confidence can only be created through a freer flow of persons, information and ideas across the dividing line.

The idea of peaceful change, first dismissed by most observers as either a naive illusion or cynical lipservice, has slowly gathered strength. What had not been foreseen by Moscow − or by Washington for that matter − was that the Helsinki Conference, originally intended to be a conclusion, turned out to be a beginning. The Final Act was not the last word. It gave birth to what in modern diplomatic jargon is called a »process». As one follow-up conference ends a new one begins, creating a White Man's UN without formal institutions and unencumbered by bureaucracy.

Since decisions are made by consensus − the right of veto belongs to each or none − the CSCE gives the smaller nations an enhanced sense of importance. For the neutral and nonaligned states it is the only international forum where they can play any role at all in the discussions on the central issues of European security. They can accordingly be relied upon to do their utmost to keep the CSCE process alive.

A »process» could be defined as a diplomatic activity that has a value in itself, even if it fails to produce immediate or tangible results. I write this without irony, for in this sense a process is the multilateral version of traditional diplomacy: the management of relations between states by peaceful means, even in the face of irreconcilable differences of interest or belief. Such differences often persist for a long time and can be softened and modified only gradually, as perceptions of national interest change.

The division of Europe is a condition likely to last a long time. Fundamentally the power structure remains frozen. Every country that during the Second World War was occupied by Germany and then liberated by the Western Allies is a member of NATO; every country that was accupied by Germany and liberated by the Soviet Union is a member of the Warsaw Pact. Outside of the two Alliances remain only the countries that had stayed out of the Second World War itself, plus three: Finland which was occupied by neither side; Yugoslavia which, though occupied by Germany, liberated itself and so retained the freedom of action enabling it to secede from the Soviet bloc; and Austria which had the good fortune of being occupied by both the Western Allies and the Soviet Union and so could be freed through a deal between the two Alliances.

Yet a balance sheet of the past twelve years must aslso take note of profound changes. The climate of opinion throughout Europe has evolved in a direction not foreseen in Helsinki. The ideological confrontation is no longer at the centre of the East-West relationship. In no country in Western Europe is Communism perceived as a threat to the existing system. Since Helsinki, parliamentary democracy has gained victo ries in Spain, Portugal and Greece. On the Eastern side, under the crust of ideological conformism differ- ences between national interest and tradition are emerging. Some of the nations in the Soviet bloc are reverting to historical type. In Poland, the regime of General Jaruzelski cannot fail to evoke memories of Marshal Pilsudski and his colonels who ran the country in the 1920s and 1930s. In Rumania, the present government by family is in the Balkan tradition. In the German Democratic Republic a systematic effort is being made to construct a national identity from el- ements of Prussian history.

After all that has happened in Eastern Europe in the past decades no one can seriously believe that the Poles or the Hungarians might join Soviet forces in an ag- gression against the West, or that the people of Czechoslovakia who for centuries have refrained from taking up arms against any one would now hurl themselves against their neighbours, or that Germans would start killing other German in the name of an ideology that has lost its appeal. A more likely threat to peace in Europe is the possibility of a break-down of political stability in Eastern Europe, which could have unforeseen and uncontrollable consequences.

For this reason maintaining a sound balance between stability and change will require skillful management. Until recently, Soviet dogmatism and centralism, in the old Russian tradition of autocracy, orthodoxy and nationalism, recoiled from every change. Today, it se- ems, Moscow recognizes that rigidity is in fact the greatest threat to stability. Change in Eastern Europe is inevitable. But how fast and how far can it go wi- thout undermining stability?

This is the crucial dilemma, not only for the Soviet

leaders, but also for the West. Western policy is designed to promote greater national independence for the Socialist states in Eastern Europe as well as greater individual freedom for the citizens in those states. But these two goals are not always compatible. In Hungary, strict adherence to the Soviet line in international affairs has bought her citizens greater freedom internally; in Rumania, orthodoxy at home has been combined with heretical gestures in foreign relations; in Poland, the suppression by military rule of demands for greater freedom for her citizens was justified as a patriotic act that preserved national independence.

Western reactions to events in Eastern Europe tend to be confused and inconsistent. On the one hand the West applauds every internal challenge to the Socialist regimes, without of course accepting responsibility for its possible consequences for the people involved. On the other hand the West rejoices every time these regimes deviate from the Soviet line, even though such deviations may in fact strengthen their position at home.

The element of hypocrisy inherent in Western policy becomes apparent the moment the German issue is touched. The real guarantee of what Moscow calls the status quo in Europe is of course the division of Germany. But no one in the West wishes to revive the issue of German reunification. The division of Germany remains the hard rock of common interest between the two blocs. Both Alliances are organized on the assumption that the division is permanent, and as each camp moves toward greater political and economic unity within itself, the division is further reinforced.

Yet the politicians and soldiers standing guard over the holy status quo may already have lost the battle without knowing it. Not ideology but technology is likely to bring about the unification of Europe. Advan-

153

ces in communications are already making a mockery of some of the traditional measures to shield nations against foreign influences. Glasnost is a function of techonological change. So is the powerful momentum of economic integration which is breaking down barriers, not only within Western Europe, but also between countries with different social systems. European unity is likely to grow, not out of the barrel of a gun, but from the seeds sown by the microchip.

XVIII
The End of the Road?

Before the Finnish people have had much chance to enjoy the security and affluence they have achieved in the 1980s, new prophets of doom have raised their voice in warning. Once again the Finns are told the end is near. This time it is not rape by Russian imperialism or enslavement by communist doctrine that is expected to put an end to the independence of Finland: She will be seduced by the bright lights of the Western world. The final chapter will be written, not in the manner of George Orwell's 1984, but rather as foreshadowed by Aldous Huxley's Brave New World. Unable to compete with the giant multinational corporations in research and development, Finland will be reduced to a new type of colonial dependency. As business becomes more and more internationalized, decisions affecting the vital economic interests of Finland will be taken by faceless managers in New York or London or Zürich. The global technostructure of finance and industry will finally render the nation state obsolete. Enfeebled by a continued brain drain and conditioned by the products of the international entertainment industry – already now the majority of Finns are able to watch several international commercial TV channels – the Finnish people will lack the intellectual resources needed to maintain their distinct cultural identity. They will cease to be a nation; they will become a group of producers and consumers living in one corner of what appropriately is called the Common Market.

By joining Europe the Finns will no doubt keep up with the Swedes and others in terms of material living standards, but at the end of the road Finland will no longer be Finland.

The threat to national identity inherent in economic integration is perceived in countries much bigger and more powerful than Finland. It has been graphically described by a French politician of the Left, Jean-Pierre Chevenement, who has written that if things go on as they are going now, by the year 2000 France will be a kind of Algeria appended to the United States: the majority of the French, »in Basque berets, their litre of red wine and their camembert in their pouches, will continue to speak French, surviving in mountain villages.»

These words were written before the socialist government in France, of which M. Chevenement himself was a member, in the early 1980s discovered it could not swim against the current prevailing in the Western economies and had to make a U-turn to bring its policies in line with those of its neighbours.

The logic of those predicting the end of the nation state is persuasive. But logic is seldom a reliable guide to the future. Obviously, economic integration creates an ever greater interdependence between states and this inevitably reduces the scope of independent action. Every country from time to time chafes under the constraints thus imposed upon it, while the advantages gained through economic integration and the opportunities it offers are taken for granted. On balance, however, it must be recognized that, in national terms, the gains outweigh the disadvantages. The independence of Finland, measured by her capacity to safeguard and promote the interests of her citizens, surely now is far greater than it was at the time the country was poor and backward and wholly dependent on the export of forest products. As a small economy, Finland has little influence on the general trends of the world economy, but within the frame set by those trends success or failure depends on her own performance – her ability to maximize the benefits of integration and minimize its negative effects. National independence has become a function of economic competitiveness.

This view is rejected by the Greens and other seekers of alternative lifestyles who believe the industrial world is heading toward a general breakdown. Why should Finland compete so strenuously for a first class passage on a ship that is bound to sink soon? They advocate a reduction of Finland's dependence on the world economy through a return to a simpler way of life which would eliminate the need to produce or import a great number of unnecessary goods and save the natural environment from further destruction.

Such a retreat from the evil world into the security of an inner citadel has been the dream of stoics and ascetics, religious men and revolutionary philosophers throughout the ages. »He is truly free,» said Rousseau, »who desires what he can perform and does what he desires.» The adherents of this ancient doctrine are likely to remain a political fringe group in Finland, but their message attracts a great deal of attention in the media which always are on the lookout for provocative critics of established policy, and it sounds vaguely appealing to those who long for some release from the strains of competitive living.

But a venomous snake lurks in paradise restored. There is an element of arrogance in the assumption that much of what is produced and consumed in our societies is unnecessary and could be eliminated. Who will decide which human needs and wants are legitimate and which unnecessary? And by what means will such decisions be enforced? A retreat to a simpler way of life would be far from idyllic. It could only be carried out through the imposition of total controls on economic and social life. At the end of that road Finland surely would no longer be Finland: it would be more like Albania.

There are no absolute or definitive answers to the complex issues raised by the rapid internationalization of economic activity in the industrial world. In the liberal view, the interests and rights of the individual must be placed at the centre of public policy. But only a very small minority of citizens in any state has the talent or the skills to make the world their stage. The best Finnish singers perform in the Metropolitan opera, the toughest icehockey players join the professional teams of the National Hockey League of the United States. The great majority of Finns, however, need the Republic of Finland to look after their interests.

Europe remains an abstraction; reality is in nations, regions, tribes and communities. As material standards and educational levels rise, people rebel against the tyranny of large-scale organizations, refusing to submit to be governed from far away. Everywhere in the industrial world the demand is for a wider participation in decision-making, not only in public administration but also in industry and business, in political parties and labour unions.

Even in ancient states like the United Kingdom, France and Spain, central government seems unable to satisfy the needs and aspirations of different minorities and regions. The Basques, the Scots, the Welsh wish to run their own lives, and their cause cannot fail to receive sympathy from the Finns who firmly believe they would never have achieved their present wealth and freedom had they remained under the rule of Stockholm or St. Petersburg or, more recently, been forced to submit to Moscow. Neither the Finns nor the other nations of Europe are likely to resign themselves to be governed from Brussels. Economic integration certainly will continue, but not to the point of national extinction.

True, Finland is being »Europeanized», for better and for worse. For better, in that it is breaking down the self- centered insularity of Finnish life; for worse, by undermining some of the old-fashioned civic virtues that still are honoured among the Finnish people. Many Finns do now watch the inane TV programmes which satellites beam around the globe. But it would be futile to try to prevent them from wasting their time in such a manner: If deprived of Dallas and Dynasty, would they devote their evenings to reading Finnish classics or listening to Sibelius?

In the cultural sphere, as in the economic, protectionism is a self-defeating policy. The cultural identity of a nation cannot be cultivated artificially, within the walls of an ethnic reservation. It must be able to survive and grow in the open. The pessimists, like Milan Kundera whom I have quoted in an earlier chapter, claim that »culture has already bowed out of Europe». I do not share this view. Material success is not in itself a victory of materialism. On the contrary, more people than ever before now have the means and the leisure to engage in cultural activities. Nor do I believe that the continued integration of the economies of the West European states will wipe out the nations and their distinct cultural indentities. There is no alternative to integration; but neither is there an alternative to the nation state. The contradiction cannot be resolved: we must live with it.

A Note of Sources

The greater part of the printed sources I have used are available only in Finnish or Swedish, and thus presumably of no interest to all but a very few of those who may read this book. I have therefore included references only to sources that exist in English. In addition to the authors and works I have referred to in the text of the book, I should mention *Finland in the 20th Century* by D.G. Kirby and *Mannerheim – Marshal of Finland* by Stig Jägerskjöld, both published by C. Hurst & Co, London.

I feel specially indebted to three Finnish scholars whose influence can be detected in parts of this book. They are Professor Matti Klinge on history, Professor Erik Allardt on social developments and Professor Jaakko Honko on economic policy.

I have also drawn freely on my own previous works, two of which are available in English: *Finland Survived* (Otava 1984), originally published in 1961 by Harvard University Press under the title *The Diplomacy of the Winter War,* and *Finnish Neutrality* (Praeger 1968).

Max Jakobson